THE
END
OF THE
AGE

SPECIFIC EVENTS LEADING TO THE LAUNCH OF THE END TIMES & THE FLOW OF END TIME EVENTS

DAVID BRENNAN, SR.

The End of the Age

Website for this book: www.SwordofDavid.com

Published by Teknon Publishing, Metairie, Louisiana

ISBN Number: 978-1-7324135-3-5

CONFESSION OF FAITH

I believe in Jesus Christ of Nazareth, placed in the womb of woman by the Spirit of God, crucified on a Roman cross nearly two thousand years ago, died, rose from the dead, and is the resurrection and the eternal life of those placing their trust and faith in Him alone. I believe He is the only way to salvation, and place my faith and trust in Him alone for the cleansing of my multitude of sins. I cannot save myself.

I believe He is the Son of the living God, true God and true man, whom the Father sent into the world on a mission of salvation for mankind, overcoming the forces of darkness through His light, guiding believers by the presence of the Holy Spirit, and working His holy will not by might nor by power, but by His Spirit.

I believe the Bible is the unerring Word of God, given mankind for salvation and guidance, written through the hand of the prophets guided by the Holy Spirit, the source of truth in a world filled with deception.

I believe all prophetic utterances in the Bible will come to pass in due time. I believe in the simplicity and literalness of His prophecies.

In Christ,
David Brennan

CONTENTS

CONTENTS

The End of the Age

The sea is a place of peace. And hope. Its murmuring waves kindle a tranquil symphony in harmony with souls walking its shore. A calming melody relaxing the human will and prying open hardened hearts. Its peace is often punctuated by crying seabirds above and on the shore small creatures running about paying little mind to the affairs of men. Too busy scurrying from small holes to the water and back to be distracted. Often the air is filled with the scent of fishermen and their catch. Their small boats pulled up on shore stalked by cats seeking an easy meal. It was in such a setting that Jesus spoke to His followers.

Like so many of His talks, this one too would become famous by a simple phrase. The "wheat and tares" parable. Words instantly recognized by any believer. When the word "multitude" is used alongside Jesus it typically means a very large group of people. Indeed, His reputation for preforming miracles was a draw like no other. Not only did excitement seekers come, but those hearing a deeper call — a yearning of the spirit. And who knew such a calling came from the Spirit of God? As a "multitude" of people stood on the shore Jesus "got into a boat and sat."

Sitting in one of the fishing boats likely created an amphitheater effect. With the crowd on the shore placed above the boat the water acted as a kind of amplifier. And as was so customary Jesus used an example of a common experience to convey a simple point. Since agriculture was a significant part of the economy, with its sewing and reaping process, that is what Jesus used to relay His message.

> [3] Then He spoke many things to them in parables, saying: "Behold, a sower went out to sow. [4] And as he sowed, some seed fell by the wayside; and the birds came and devoured them. [5] Some fell on stony places, where they did not have much earth; and they immediately sprang up because they had no depth of earth. [6] But when the sun was up they were scorched, and because they had no root they withered away. [7] And some fell among thorns, and the thorns sprang up and choked them. [8] But others fell on good ground and yielded a crop: some a hundredfold, some sixty, some thirty. [9] He who has ears to hear, let him hear!" Matthew 13:3-9

Certainly, those listening had encountered varied experiences in life of fortune and failure. The shared reality of a diversity of results. After telling a story that all could relate to Jesus explained its spiritual significance. It related to the gathering of truth into the hearts of men. For some, it would stay safely tucked away for all eternity producing a bounty of good in their earthly life. But for most, it would perish by one means or another. And typically who was behind this perishing was the devil.

The accusation leveled by Jesus against the wicked one is multifold. Sometimes his filthy hands snatched away the seed of life the moment it was planted. Finding unfortunate success all too often. For others, the growth of a wondrous sprout is smothered to death before it can take deep root. But if the dark one fails to stop it before it takes root then he has another plan. He always seems to have a plan.

When sprouting roots appear within a heart then demonic influence comes into play. Seeking to harden it into a heart of stone so the spreading roots can reach no deeper. And typically the offshoot dies before producing fruit. Or the offshoot might be dealt with by another means. That means usually involves the use of thorns scattered about to choke it to death. Thorns do that. But there is always that seed that finds good ground taking deep root and producing a rich crop. A harvest of "wheat."

The foul beast hates "wheat." It is his bitter enemy. Having failed to stop the production of "wheat" there is only one thing left for him to do. Sow "tares among" it. Here is the story of that wicked deed.

> [24] Another parable He put forth to them, saying: "The kingdom of heaven is like a man who sowed good seed in his field; [25] but while men slept, his enemy came and sowed tares among the wheat and went his way. [26] But when the grain had sprouted and produced a crop, then the tares also appeared. [27] So the servants of the owner came and said to him, 'Sir, did you not sow good seed in your field? How then does it have tares?' [28] He said to them, 'An enemy has done this.' The servants said to him, 'Do you want us then to go and gather them up?' Matthew 13:24-28

This "wheat" is coveted by the Lord. Having sprinkled it with His blood it is His church. And there is no dark plan He cannot overcome in Divine wisdom. Since uprooting the "tares" sewn among the "wheat" could seriously disrupt His crop He bides His time. He will deal with them on His terms. At the "harvest."

> [29] But he said, 'No, lest while you gather up the tares you also uproot the wheat with them. [30] Let both grow to-gether until the <u>harvest</u>, and at the time of <u>harvest</u> I will say to the reapers, "First gather together the tares and bind them in bundles to burn them, but gather the wheat into my barn." Matthew 13:29-30

Like any good master, He takes great care with what he values most. His "wheat" is precious to Him. He patiently waits until the "harvest" and only then allows the "tares" to be dealt with. Although uprooting the "tares" sewn between the "wheat" will disrupt His precious crop it doesn't matter at the "harvest." Because the "wheat" is to then be taken anyway.

Like all of His parables, this one too has a much deeper meaning. His explanation provides an answer to one of the most pressing questions in the cosmos. Why is there such evil among men? Part of it can be explained by these "tares" and their tare-isms. Hearts devoured with evil and hardened in thickets of thorns. But it is Jesus' explanation of the parable that catches our attention. In it, He uses a phrase to describe the time wherein His "wheat" is taken off the earth.

[37] He answered and said to them: "He who sows the good seed is the Son of Man. [38] The field is the world, the good seeds are the sons of the kingdom, but the tares are the sons of the wicked one. [39] The enemy who sowed them is the devil, the harvest is <u>the end of the age</u>, and the reapers are the angels. [40] Therefore as the tares are gathered and burned in the fire, so it will be at <u>the end of this age</u>. [41] The Son of Man will send out His angels, and they will gather out of His kingdom all things that offend, and those who practice lawlessness, [42] and will cast them into the furnace of fire. There will be wailing and gnashing of teeth. [43] Then the righteous will shine forth as the sun in the kingdom of their Father. He who has ears to hear, let him hear! Matthew 13:37-43

The example of the "wheat" and "tares" relates to the most supernatural event the world will ever see. The resurrection of the dead and the rapture. The taking of His church out of the world ending the church age. "The end of the age." His beloved prophet Daniel spoke of the same describing it with a slight variation — "the end of the days." A distinction without a difference.

This book relays the prophetic story concerning the culmination of this grand cosmic battle called the end times. Looking at the events that must transpire just before it begins as well as those when it unfolds. It is based on a literal reading of the prophets who spoke and wrote about it.

CHAPTER ONE

Warnings Signs: A War & Heavenly Wonders

There is a day coming when something very strange will appear in the heavens above the earth. Perhaps the scene will invoke the use of a comet or a stray asteroid in a fantastic and frightening orbit. Or possibly it will be an inexplicable atmospheric condition producing an unusual light display in the sky. Perhaps it will only be seen at night. Perhaps not. Science will try to explain it, but will likely fail. We can only speculate as to what form it will take. Will strange lights flicker above? Or will it be akin to the northern lights, but more widespread? About it, we only know what the prophet Joel tells us. And he is vague. But speculate we must as this is part of the cosmic warning signs that will appear just before the dreaded end times begin. In his own words...

> And I will show wonders in the heavens and in the earth:
> Blood and fire and pillars of smoke. Joel 2:30

Joel leaves us to speculate as to what those "wonders in the heavens" will be. In fact, the Hebrew word used for "wonders" is the masculine noun "mopet" a word typically used for that of a "miracle." For example, "mopet" was used in the Book of Exodus to depict the plagues sent against

Pharaoh. And certainly, from the perspective of the Egyptians and the Israelites, those plagues were miracles. So whatever these wonders in the heavens are they will be viewed by men on earth as some kind of miracle occurring in the heavens above. Something extraordinary and highly unusual. For now, we can only imagine what they will be. But there is one thing Joel does not leave to the imagination. Something on the earth will accompany these heavenly miracles. War. And a notable one at that. How do we know it will be notable? Not only because it ranks to be placed in prophecy scripture, but because this particular war will possess a terrifying uniqueness.

There are certain ancient Biblical prophecies that in the modern age take on new meaning due to the evolution of language and knowledge. And in this case, Joel's words appear to be one such example. Across the ages, the words "in the earth: Blood and fire and pillars of smoke" would have easily been understood to signify warfare. That is true. But ancient man could not fully appreciate the details of Joel's war description. That knowledge was reserved for modern man. Considering that both fire as well as pillars of smoke are the descriptions given for this war then modern knowledge points us in a certain direction.

There are several notable characteristics associated with the detonation of a nuclear weapon. And today every adult person instantly recognizes them. Upon igniting there is a fireball. It has been called a fireball since the inception of the grim bomb. The fireball consists of massive waves of swirling firestorms and writhing flames the like of which are incomparable on the earth. This notable characteristic shares top billing with another trait. The mushroom cloud. But there is another way of saying it. Pillars of smoke. Eventually, the fireball transforms into a cloud of smoke that forms a mushroom-shaped pillar marking the final remains of the detonation. And also marking the final remains of countless souls who were instantly vaporized.

What is interesting about these pillars of smoke is the specific Hebrew word used in describing them. It is "timara." Whereas we typically think of pillars of smoke as being straight upright ones such as those supporting a building. The word "timara" depicts pillars of smoke comparable to that of a palm tree. A wide top sitting above a narrow stem. The exact definition of "timara," according to Strong's Concordance, is that of a palm-like spreading at the top. Consider the pictures comparing a typical palm tree to the mushroom cloud of a nuclear blast. The common shape is undeniable.

Whether or not Joel is referring to nuclear or conventional bombs only time will tell. But based on the unique characteristics of nuclear detonations including fire (fireball) and pillars of smoke with a palm-like spreading at the top nuclear detonations would appear to be a very strong candidate to fulfill his words. As for the second heavenly warning sign, it is very direct as well.

> 31 The sun shall be turned into darkness, And the moon
> into blood, Before the coming of the great and awesome
> day of the LORD. Joel 2:31

Straight forward we are told the sun will darken and the moon shall be turned to blood. The moon will not literally turn into blood. It will turn red in color. Since this is a major sign that "the day of the Lord" is about to begin, this heavenly sign also must be notable. Exactly what form this sign in the sun and moon will take we are not told. It possibly will be some kind of notable solar eclipse and blood moon. However, when this heavenly warning takes place, in conjunction with the wonders in the heavens and its notable war, a clear and positive identification can be made. The end times are about to begin.

Some say the sun darkening and the moon turning to blood are the wonders spoken of in the previous verse. Although possible it would appear unlikely for a couple of reasons. Spread out across scripture are a multitude of references to the sun and moon associated with the day of the Lord and never are they described as wonders in the heavens. Additionally, the heavenly event of the sun darkening and a blood moon are not uncommon. And they are certainly not considered miracles in line with the Hebrew word "mopet" used to describe these wonders in the heavens.

Unfortunately, the effort to identify the notable war associated with these wonders in the heavens is complicated by the fact that Joel does not name the nations involved in it. For that matter not so much as a hint is given. All we know is that this war is a major warning sign that the day of the Lord — the end times — is about to begin. And it may involve nuclear detonations. Now some speculation is necessary. Speculation and not certainty since the nations involved in the war are not named.

The case will be presented here that this strange war will involve Israel and not the nations in general. And the nation most likely to be their adversary — the one that best fulfills various scriptures — modern-day Iran. But there is also the possibility that this war could involve nations other than Israel. However, such a scenario would leave many prophetic loose ends dangling. Of course, the final word on this war will be the clear identifier of some kind of miracles or wonders in the heavens that will accompany it. Let me say that again. This war will be identified when there is a notable war with palm tree-shaped (mushroom clouds) smoke clouds and fire deeply associated with it along with some form of wonders or miracles occurring in the sky alongside it. Here is the case that Israel is the nation that fits best being involved in this war.

As the case for Israel is presented follow the scriptures with care. Their details will be taken literally so as to eliminate the passions of men as much as possible. We will start with the words of Jesus. In His Olivet Discourse Jesus provided details on wars happening just before the day of the Lord begins. As a result of the specific details that He provides, certain logical deductions that can be made as to the identity of the nations involved in Joel's notable war based on current geopolitical conditions.

Jesus' Wars and rumors of wars

When looking into Bible prophecy it is always helpful to find a solid reference point from which to move forward. The prophet Joel provides one by telling us these two heavenly warning signs will take place just before the day of the Lord begins. So the reference point he provides relates to the time frame just before the day of the Lord starts. And the beginning of the day of the Lord is the beginning of the end times. The day of the Lord is the end time from start to finish. As we move along you'll see why this has to be true based strictly on a simplistic and literal reading of scripture. Therefore, understand that the term the day of the Lord and the term end times will be used interchangeably. The term end times is simply the popular way of saying "the day of the Lord." But before connecting Joel's warning signs coming just before the day of the Lord to Jesus' Olivet Discourse, we first need to take a slight detour. That detour is to establish that there are two types of prophetic birth pangs.

There are general birth pangs and specific birth pangs. General birth pangs are the type mentioned in Romans 8 whereby… "²²We know that the whole creation groans and labors with birth pangs together until now." And these birth pangs appear to be rapidly accelerating in our day. But it is the specific birth pangs we will focus on. They are a technical term representing the literal start of the day of the Lord. This is established by a literal reading of various scriptures. This detour is brief but necessary.

End Time Birth Pangs

These specific end time birth pangs take place just before the birth of
the seven-year tribulation. It would be difficult to find a student of Bible
prophecy who thought prophetic birth pangs take place in a time frame
after the beginning. The thought of birth pangs happening after a birth
collapses from the weight of its absurdity. Birth pangs happen before the
birth of something. In Bible prophecy, birth pangs lead up to the birth of
the seven-year tribulation. They do not happen after it starts. This is common sense. A woman does not go to the hospital, experiences the birth of
a baby girl, and a year later begins experiencing birth pangs. They happen
before the little one arrives.

In the Old Testament when speaking to prophetic birth pangs the
Hebrew word "yalad" is used. In the New Testament, it is the Greek
verb "oden." Consider the implications of Paul's usage of birth pangs in 1
Thessalonians 5:1-3. These verses establish that the beginning of the day
of the Lord is the beginning of the end times. It also references a "Peace"
agreement. More on that in the next chapter.

> But concerning the times and the seasons, brethren, you
> have no need that I should write you. For you yourselves
> know perfectly that the day of the Lord so comes as a
> thief in the night. For when they say, "Peace and safety!"
> then sudden destruction comes upon them, as labor pains
> upon a pregnant woman. And they shall not escape. 1
> Thessalonians 5:1-3

The Greek verb "oden" is used here when speaking of "labor pains upon
a pregnant woman" to identify prophetic birth pangs. And what event is
this? It is the "sudden destruction" beginning of the day of the Lord. Paul
is letting us know that the beginning of the day of the Lord is birth pangs.
Those specific birth pangs. This is why the statement was previously made
that the beginning of the day of the Lord marks the beginning of what is

popularly called the end times. There is no beginning to the end times before these specific birth pangs and we were just told the start of the day of the Lord are these birth pangs. They are the birth pangs beginning phase of the day of the Lord which happens just before the seven-year tribulation starts. Birth pangs birth the seven years. And since Zechariah 14 tells us it is still the day of the Lord when Jesus steps foot on the Mount of Olives at the very end of the seven-year tribulation, then we know the day of the Lord has to span the entire length of the end times. Paul so simplistically presents birth pangs here as launching the day of the Lord (end times) that no question should remain. This confirms that the notable war with the possible use of nuclear weapons, in conjunction with wonders in the heavens, does in fact, take place just before the end times begin. Now back to Joel.

Remember Joel identified two heavenly signs coming just before the beginning of the day of the Lord. The first was described as wonders in the heavens with a notable war on the earth. And it is that notable war we are looking to get a better handle on. Since Paul told us the actual beginning of the day of the Lord are these specific prophetic birth pangs, now we will look at Jesus' opening descriptions of the end times in His Olivet Discourse which He too describes as birth pangs. That will then allow us to isolate certain events Jesus tells us will happen before the day of the Lord starts just as Joel did in describing the notable war associated with wonders in the heavens. The pre-birth pangs events Jesus describes will add to our knowledge of Joel's notable war and lead to logical speculation as to the nations involved in that war.

Jesus' Olivet Discourse is found in Matthew 24, Luke 21, and Mark 13, and in it, the Savior takes the reader from the beginning of the end times to the end. But we are only concerned with the beginning here as we seek to isolate events just before it starts. We will focus on Matthew's account.

> [6] And you will hear of wars and rumors of wars. See that you are not troubled; for all these things must come to pass, but the end is not yet.

7 For nation will rise against nation, and kingdom against kingdom. And there will be famines, pestilences, and earthquakes in various places. 8 All these are the beginning of sorrows. Matthew 24:6-8

Follow this carefully. Notice how Jesus makes a clear distinction between the events described in verse 6 from those in verses 7 and 8. In verse 6 He describes a time of "wars and rumors of wars," but flatly says they are nothing to be "troubled" about as "the end is not yet." In other words "the end" times have not yet started. But in verse 7 His tone completely changes. In it, He describes nations and kingdoms rising to war accompanied by "famines, pestilences, and earthquakes in various places." Whereas the events in verse 6 were nothing to be "troubled" about, in verse 7 He says "All these are the beginning of sorrows." Big difference. The word used to denote the "beginning" is the Greek verb "oden." Birth pangs. Jesus describes the events in verse 7 as the birth pangs moment of the end times. And He says these birth pangs are the beginning. Keep in mind these are specific birth pangs as opposed to the general ones that have been taking place for some time now. And we know from Paul in 1 Thessalonians 5:1-3 prophetic birth pangs (Greek verb "oden") mark the "sudden destruction" starting of the day of the Lord. The beginning. The Greek "oden" is interchangeably used for both birth pangs and the beginning. Because birth pangs are the beginning of the day of the Lord. The end times.

Therefore, the events Jesus describes in verse 7 have to also mark the beginning of the day of the Lord. The Spirit is consistent. Now we know the events in verse 6 must relate to what will happen just before the day of the Lord starts. And this places those events in the same time frame as Joel's notable war which also happens just before the day of the Lord begins. Now take careful notice that there is a certain logical contradiction relating to the wars mentioned in verse 6 if they are applied to the nations at large. And this contradiction is a small detail that is critically informative.

We are told in verse 7 that the nations and kingdoms of the earth will have to "rise" to war against each other when it begins. This is the same sudden destruction described in 1 Thessalonians 5:1-3 that begins the day of the Lord. Since they must rise to war when verse 7 arrives, then they cannot already be involved in significant wars against each other before that verse. Because if they were already involved in significant wars, then they would not be able to rise to warfare in verse 7. This is a detail of scripture that is frequently missed. Therefore, generally speaking, the nations must be quietly settled down in verse 6 in order to rise to warfare when verse 7 arrives.

But since verse 6 talks about wars notable enough to be placed in scripture as already taking place, then this appears to tell us that those wars in verse 6 do not apply to the nations of the earth. Otherwise, verses 6 and 7 experience that logical contradiction: How can the nations rise to notable warfare in verse 7 if they are already involved in notable warfare in verse 6? And the answer is, of course, they cannot. Therefore, it would appear likely that the wars of verse 6 do not relate to the nations across the earth. And since scripture is divided between Israel on the one hand, and all other nations on the other hand, then the only remaining option is that those wars must relate to Israel. And if that is the case then the logical contradiction is eliminated.

Since the wars of verse 6 take place just before the day of the Lord starts, we can understand they likely relate to Israel, and we know Joel's notable war associated with wonders in the heavens also takes place just before the day of the Lord starts, then it is likely Joel's notable war involves Israel. So it would appear that Joel's notable war involving the possible use of nuclear weapons, associated with those wonders in the heavens, all occurring just before the day of the Lord (end times) begins will likely involve the restored state of Israel. This is speculation but you may agree there is a logic to it that does not fit if other nations are used to replace Israel. And Israel is a nation that happens to possess quite an arsenal of nukes. But who is it that Israel is fighting? To that question, we can further speculate by making another logical deduction.

Since the wars of Matthew 24:6 likely involve Israel, then the rumors of wars mentioned in the verse should also apply to the Jewish state. Consider the verse again.

> [6] And you will hear of wars and <u>rumors of wars</u>. See that you are not troubled; for all these things must come to pass, but the end is not yet. Matthew 24:6

It is a modern-day fact that Israel has experienced more wars and rumors of wars than any other nation since its rebirth in the year 1948. The most notable rumor has been rummaging about since the year 2000 involving a war with Iran and its proxy allies over its nuclear weapons program. Israel views that program as an existential threat. And rightfully so. The Iranian leadership has indicated on multiple occasions an intention to destroy the restored Jewish state in a second Holocaust. As for the Jews, they promise "never again." This scenario has produced persistent rumors of wars between Israel on one side, and Iran and her proxy allies on the Israeli border on the other.

Based on their history of experiencing pogroms, persecutions, and the Holocaust, it is probably safe to say that the Jewish people will do whatever it takes to prevent Iran from engulfing them in the flames of destruction. And Iran's refusal to give up its nuclear weapons program, despite of writhing economic and diplomatic sanctions, evidences a dark agenda guided by a grim and grisly moral compass. It is likely this observation is not lost on Israeli leadership. Consider a particularly pregnant scenario concerning the two nations.

At some point, Israeli intelligence will inform their leadership that the Iranian nuclear program has finally arrived at the cusp of being able to mass produce nuclear weapons. Combined with the Iranian advanced rocket program, a black assessment for the survival of Israel will be embraced. And this will present Israeli leadership with a Hobson's choice. Either they take extreme action or none at all. This stark choice is born from the fact that the Iranian nuclear program is housed hundreds of feet below mountains of granite making only the most extreme military option sufficient in dealing with it. By protecting their facilities in this way it is clear the Persians learned the lesson of the Iraqi and Syrian nuclear programs. Both were destroyed by Israeli air units before they could spawn bombs. Both were built on the surface.

Although there are very powerful conventional weapons that can blast into granite rock. To reach the depths necessary to disable a program located so deep would require repeated such bombs dropped over the same spot. One after another burrowing their way through disheveled heaps of granite to the necessary depths. However, this would expose Israeli air units to the excellent Iranian air defense systems provided to them by the Russians. Not only would Israeli losses be great, but there would be little assurance that the targets were destroyed. Having just been attacked the Iranians would then have justification to use any weapon at their disposal to ward off the "aggressor." And there is the Hobson's choice. Israel can choose to do nothing and face possible annihilation. Or they can choose the dire option of using tactical nuclear weapons against all targets simultaneously to ensure their destruction. If this analysis is correct they will opt for the second choice of using nuclear-tipped cruise missiles on submarines positioned in the Persian Gulf. Only this one action would ensure the complete destruction of every Iranian nuclear site and fulfill prophecy scripture if it coincides with some form of miracles or wonders in the heavens. This is why it is no coincidence that Iran's "red line" with Israel is the entry of Jewish state nuclear submarines into the Persian Gulf. The Persians who invented the game of chess have identified Israel's check-mate move.

In determining if it is nuclear or conventional weapons Joel's notable war is identifying it must be pointed out that bunker buster bombs do not produce a debris cloud comparable to a palm tree or mushroom cloud. And the prophecy of Joel is clear. It will be palm tree-shaped pillars of smoke associated with this war. Nor do bunker-busting bombs produce a fireball comparable to that of other conventional weapons due to the detonation taking place under the surface. Consider the scripture again.

"And I will show wonders in the heavens and in the earth:
Blood and fire and pillars of smoke. Joel 2:30

As noted previously the words fire and pillars of smoke have two characteristics of nuclear detonations. The fireball fulfills the fire part of the verse, and the mushroom cloud fulfills the pillars of smoke part. This is because the Hebrew word "timara" is used for pillars indicates a palm tree spreading on top of a narrow stem. Both are fulfilled by a nuclear detonation. However, neither is fulfilled by a bunker-buster bomb.

The typical bunker-buster bomb explosion on the left is distinctly different from that of the nuclear explosion depicted on the right. Whereas the bunker buster does not fulfill the words of Joel, a nuclear detonation perfectly does.

Not only would such a war between Israel and Iran put an end to the ongoing "rumors of wars" between Israel and another nation, high-lighting Matthew 24:6 and its rumors of wars, but a transition would take place from rumors to actual warfare. Both are indicated in the verse as taking place before the day of the Lord begins. The use of tactical nuclear weapons would also produce a war with the fire and pillars of smoke foretold by Joel as happening in the same pre-day of the Lord time frame. Of course, the war would have to be accompanied by some kind of wonders in the heavens to be confirmed as the one mentioned by Joel. Such a war would certainly be a notable one in the record of warfare. But such a war would set the stage for the next geopolitical event, also indicated in prophetic scriptures, to take place just before the day of the Lord begins.

THE END OF THE AGE

CHAPTER TWO

When They Say Peace

Men typically seek their own will over that of others. And often terrible brutality is employed to accomplish it. The time leading up to the launch of "the day of the Lord" will be no different. A moment is coming when men will declare pious platitudes of Peace. But as they do so destruction will lurk in the savage hearts of many. Soon to produce magnums of tears across a deceived world. It will be the cold winter of men's hearts just before writhing destruction visits their nations.

Should Israel use tactical nuclear weapons in defending herself from the mortal threat that is the Iranian nuclear program she will become the ultimate pariah state. The children of Holocaust survivors will face a united front of nations accusing them of the same. As a result, the world will seek to extract its pound of flesh from the Jewish state for using the forbidden weapon against their foe. And they will soon get it. But according to the prophets in so doing the day of the Lord will launch turning their nations into twisted hulks and charred ruins.

Punishing Israel

According to the scriptures, the world will engage in a very specific action against Israel. And what they do will represent the final straw — or warning — just before the day of the Lord begins. In 1 Thessalonians 5:1-3 we are told about a Peace agreement just before the day of the Lord starts. Other scriptures strongly infer that this Peace agreement includes the removal of land from the Jews. Land referred to as the Promised Land due to the Lord deeding it to them in a Divine act. The Creator of the Universe created the earth and every parcel of land therein. Therefore, He can deed to whomever He wishes any land on the planet. In scripture, He deeded the area known as Palestine to the Jews.

As the words of various prophets are considered it will become obvious who it is that forces this Peace agreement on Israel. It should also be noted that this Peace agreement is being forced on Israel after the notable war adding to the case that it is Israel involved in that war and that the Peace agreement removing land is retribution. But why would retribution be directed against Israel for that particular war? Israel has been involved in countless wars with its neighbors and none have united the nations of the world to the point of forcing a Peace agreement on her that removes land. This infers that something happens during the notable war that shocks the world into action. Is it the use of tactical nuclear weapons by Israel? Producing the fire and pillars of smoke foretold by Joel?

The Peace Agreement—Who Does It?

As mentioned previously 1 Thessalonians 5:1-3 tells of a Peace agreement just before the day of the Lord begins. And then clearly spells out the result. Sudden destruction. We know this destruction marks the beginning of the day of the Lord because Paul tells us it is birth pangs. The end times will have begun. In describing this Peace Paul indicates those saying it will be many. Likewise, he indicates those receiving destruction will also be many. Consider his writings again focusing on the underlined words.

But concerning the times and the seasons, brethren, you have no need that I should write to you. ² For you yourselves know perfectly that the day of the Lord so comes as a thief in the night. ³For when <u>they</u> say, "Peace and safety!" then sudden destruction comes upon <u>them</u>, as labor pains upon a pregnant woman. And <u>they</u> shall not escape. 1 Thessalonians 5:1-3

Three times Paul refers to those involved in this Peace just before the day of the Lord begins in the plural. "They, them," and "they." And Paul is not alone in doing so. The prophet Daniel also refers to an agreement involving a plurality of nations.

> Then <u>he</u> shall confirm a <u>covenant with many</u> for one week;
> But in the middle of the week
> He shall bring an end to sacrifice and offering...
> Daniel 9:27

The "he" in the verse that Daniel is referring to is the Antichrist. What he does is confirm a particular agreement. The word for confirm is the Hebrew verb "gabar." According to Strong's Concordance, this word is used to indicate a strengthening of something or simply to confirm something already in place. Daniel is telling us the Antichrist shall confirm an agreement previously made. The bad man does not initiate the agreement. But he shall confirm it. And when he does so the seven-year tribulation begins. The birth pangs beginning of the day of the Lord launches from that first agreement. The dark seven years known as Daniel's 70ᵗʰ week launches when the Antichrist shall confirm that first agreement. Effectively, the tumultuous beginning phase of the day of the Lord called birth pangs leads up to the birth of those seven years. Birth pangs lead to a birth.

Notice the main characteristic of the agreement he shall confirm. It is described as "a covenant with many." Like Paul the prophet Daniel indicates a plurality of nations are involved in making the initial Peace agreement. But who is this group of nations that both Paul and Daniel speak of who initiates the agreement? The one the Antichrist later shall confirm. Knowing who it is would help to identify this all-important agreement at the time it happens. And this is critically important because that first agreement launches the beginning of the day of the Lord. Birth pangs. We find the answer to that question in the words of the prophets Joel and Jeremiah. Joel first.

After describing the two heavenly warning signs that will unfold just before the day of the Lord begins, only a few verses later Joel begins describing why that horrific time launches. As he does so he points to a certain group of nations whose unholy actions against the land of Israel result in the Lord's punishment. The launch of the day of the Lord. The birth pangs beginning phase.

> ² I will also gather <u>all nations,</u>
> And bring them down to the Valley of Jehoshaphat;
> And I will enter into judgment with them there
> On account of My people, My heritage Israel,
> Whom they have scattered among the nations;
> <u>They have also divided up My land.</u> Joel 3:2-3

Joel describes this opening shot of the end times as punishment against "all nations" and it is delivered in a place referred to as the "Valley of Jehoshaphat" — a phrase used to describe the theatre of God's judgment against "all nations." Only a few verses later Joel will use that same phrase again for a later judgment — the Battle of Armageddon — the final act of the Lord against all nations. The Valley of Jehoshaphat is simply used as an end time book-end marking both the beginning and the end of the Lord's judgments against all nations. (This simple truth should not be overcomplicated.) The initial destruction delivered against all nations at the launch of the day of the Lord — and the ending destruction against them at the Battle of "Armageddon" at the conclusion of the day of the Lord. Joel gives the reason for this opening shot against all nations: it is because "they have also divided up my land." Joel is letting us know that the dividing of the land of Israel is the reason all nations are being punished. Thus it is all nations that do the dividing which is the reason both Paul and Daniel use the plural when speaking about the same Peace agreement.

But notice that Joel does not tell us all nations use warfare to accomplish the removal. Not any indication of it. Yet, throughout the Bible when Israel suffers armed conflict it is noted. But not here. So it is not warfare that all nations use to remove the land. Which leaves only one other method. An agreement of some kind. And this lines up with Paul telling us they will say Peace just before the destruction of "the day of the Lord" begins. And that destruction matches up with the judgment of destruction visited upon all nations in the Valley of Jehoshaphat. This is why Joel does not mention warfare as the means all nations use to remove the land. And, of course, Daniel also tells us it will be the "covenant (agreement) with many" (all nations) which the Antichrist will confirm — not initiate. All happening just before the day of the Lord begins. So it is easy to see that it is all nations that do the dividing — the United Nations — the world organization that has been hot on the trail of dividing Israel for decades.

An Israeli use of tactical nuclear weapons to destroy select Iranian nuclear sites would unite a United Nations already tilted against the Jews. Under such a scenario those nations that have been standing with Israel in preventing the creation of a Palestinian state in the heart of the Biblical Promised Land step aside allowing the dark deed to finally happen. After all, it was the United Nations who crafted the initial borders of Israel from a map of raw land known as British Palestine. As such they will simply be correcting that map according to their will. Although Israel will undoubtedly be under grave pressure not to resist, due to the weight of it being "all nations" aligned against her, it will be a calamity for the Jews to give in. That is because long ago the Lord promised to restore them to their land. And they were restored. As such they should simply place their trust in Him, refuse the raging will of "all nations," and stand firm. But they will not. As a result, they will share in the Lord's wrath. But to a lesser degree as noted by the prophet Jeremiah.

The story Jeremiah tells is both fascinating and unfortunate when read within the context of the array of scriptures we have just looked at. Having seen one scripture after another either flatly state or infer a Peace agreement removing land from Israel — just before the day of the Lord begins — Jeremiah will add some very interesting details about this future event. An event so significant to story of mankind.

Paul in 1 Thessalonians 5:1-3 provided a good reference point wherein he told us the beginning of the day of the Lord is the beginning of the end times. He did that by telling us the "sudden destruction" marking the beginning represents prophetic birth pangs. Those specific birth pangs and not the general ones that have been accelerating. And, of course, these specific prophetic birth pangs take place at the beginning of what is popularly called the end times. Upon that precept, we find Jeremiah also referencing prophetic birth pangs granting us the assurance that the events he describes are also in the beginning phase of the day of the Lord. The Holy Spirit is consistent. At one point Jeremiah will colorfully refer to these events as "the time of Jacobs trouble." An apparent reference to the troubles facing Israel. And the reason for this additional description soon comes out.

The Old Testament word for "of childbirth" is the Hebrew verb "yalad." Now consider Jeremiah's usage of it in the following verses.

> [6] Ask now, and see.
> Whether a man is ever in labor with child?
> So why do I see every man with his hands on his loins
> Like a woman in labor,
> And all faces turned pale? Jeremiah 30:6

"Like a woman in labor" — birth pangs. It is the beginning of the day of the Lord. Next, he will describe the fate of all nations. Jeremiah is referring to the same all nations as Joel does. He simply adds a fuller picture of the beginning events as well as the events leading up to it.

¹¹ For I am with you,' says the LORD, 'to save you;
Though I make a <u>full end of all nations</u> where I have
scattered you. Yet I will not make a complete end of you.
But <u>I will correct you in justice</u>,
And will not let you go altogether unpunished.'
Jeremiah 30:11

All nations are brought to a "full end." Severe punishment. However, Israel is also being punished but not to the "complete end" that all nations experience. The Lord says to Israel: "I will not make a complete end of you. But I will correct you in justice." Why is Israel being punished but not as severely as all nations? The reason comes out a few verses later. All nations — the United Nations — do something to Israel that the Jewish state chooses not to resist.

¹⁶ 'Therefore all those who <u>devour</u> you shall be devoured;
And all your adversaries, every one of them, shall go
into captivity;
Those who <u>plunder</u> you shall become plunder,
And all who <u>prey upon</u> you I will make a prey. Jeremiah
30:16

All nations... "devour" Israel, they "plunder" her, and they "prey upon" her. But nowhere are we told they invade and conquer her. Israel is devoured meaning her land is taken. And the price all nations pay — they are brought to a "full end" and are themselves devoured. If this sounds familiar it should. This is essentially the same description Joel provides concerning the punishment all nations receive in his first reference to the Valley of Jehoshaphat — the valley of God's judgments against all nations during the end times. Both Jeremiah and Joel tell of all nations receiving great Godly wrath at the beginning of the day of the Lord as a result of removing/devouring land from Israel. Since neither prophet mentions warfare as the method used to remove the land we can understand it takes place through an agreement of some kind. And this places it perfectly in context with Daniel's covenant with many and Paul's when they say Peace. Because these events described by Daniel, Paul, Joel and Jeremiah all occur just before the day of the Lord begins they fit together because they are all connected.

Israel is bullied by all nations (The United Nations) into giving up land as part of a Peace agreement just before the end times begin. And this whole affair may be retribution for the notable war with those wonders in the heavens. The likely reason that particular war produces such an extreme reaction from the United Nations — unlike any of the countless other wars Israel has engaged in with her neighbors — is that something extraordinary takes place. This leads us back to the fire and pillars of smoke associated with that notable war that is shaped like a palm tree. A mushroom cloud.

Additionally, it should be observed that the Lord does not punish Israel for defending her land against armed attack. This is because He promised they would be restored to the land. And they were. Yet, in Jeremiah 30 He is punishing her and describing that punishment as the time of Jacob's trouble. All of this adds to the case that the removal must be accomplished by peaceful means. One in which Israel goes along with forgetting the promise of the land by the Lord and richly earning His punishment. But limited in comparison to that which befalls all nations.

This is why Israel also faces the Lord's wrath. But restrained. "In justice." They go along with the removal of their land without offering military resistance. And the reason why is obvious. They face the horrifying choice of going against all nations. A daunting prospect in the natural. But it is a sad day for Israel. Trading land for Peace they lose both. And the Lord's more measured response is likely due to the forces arrayed against the Jews. A unified United Nations. This is why the added reference time of Jacob's trouble is used. It is a troubling time for Israel caused of their lack of faith. But it is a much worse time for all nations.

It was the Lord who promised to restore Israel to her ancient lands. But poor secular Israel will not understand when the time arrives. They miss the opportunity for the miracle of deliverance from their God. The same God who years earlier parted the Red Sea for their ancestors. And that parting of waters was to create a pathway for the twelve tribes to make their way to some of the same lands modern Israel will give up without a fight.

Three Major Warning Signs Before Specific Birth Pangs Launch

The start of the day of the Lord, popularly known as the end times, will launch the most difficult time in human history. Yet, there are three major warning signs in scripture before it begins. When Paul tells of the sudden destruction that begins the day of the Lord, he tells us to watch and be sober indicating a duty to be aware.

> [4] But you, brethren, are not in darkness, so that this Day should overtake you as a thief. [5] You are all sons of light and sons of the day. We are not of the night nor of darkness. [6] Therefore let us not sleep, as others do, but let us watch and be sober. 1 Thessalonians 5:4-6

Since the "sons of light" are not in "darkness" they are to "watch and be sober" for the day of the Lord. If this means anything it is that there are signs to watch for. And as we have seen three major ones that are specific and clear.

We know from Joel some kind of strange wonders in the heavens will unfold just as a notable war is taking place on earth. These wonders will likely be viewed by men as miracles in the sky. And the reason for the war being notable may be because it involves the limited use of nuclear weapons. The first angry use of an atom-splitting bomb since two were dropped on Japan in 1945. This would fulfill the fire and pillars of smoke foretold by the prophet. The fireball and mushroom cloud. It appears that Israel, which happens to possess a significant nuclear arsenal, is the most likely candidate to fulfill this prophecy. They are the nation that has suffered more wars and rumors of wars than any other country since its rebirth in 1948. And because rumors of wars are a notable sign added by Jesus in His Olivet Discourse, another condition just before the day of the Lord begins, this raises the specter that the other nation involved in Joel's notable war will be Iran and her proxy allies on the Israeli border. Its nuclear threat to Israel producing raging rumors of impending warfare between the two nations since the year 2000. This is all speculation but based on geopolitical events and logical inference from literal scripture. Such an attack by the Jewish state would both horrify and unify the world.

The unification of the world would be toward one common goal: making Israel pay for the attack. And other than outright invasion of her — which would no doubt be rejected by many countries — the next best option would be to remove some of her lands for the creation of a Palestinian state and the delusion of Peace. An abomination placed directly in the heart of the Promised Land — so called for the ancient prophecies foretelling its return to the Jews. But also a goal of the ungodly United Nations for decades.

It is clear from an array of prophets that no single nation will pull off the Peace agreement removing her land. It will take a united effort on the part of the only world body on earth representing all nations perfectly fulfilling the words of the prophets. The United Nations. Such an action will be the last straw breaking the back of the prophetic end-time camel. All that will remain at that point is the final warning that the day of the Lord is about to start. The birth pangs beginning of the day of the Lord.

Joel is clear and specific concerning this warning. "The sun shall be turned into darkness, and the moon into blood, before the coming of the great and awesome day of the Lord." And so it shall be! Exactly what form this takes can be speculated upon. But it will happen only after the first two signs take place removing the possibility of a misreading.

Then Specific Birth Pangs Begin

At the conclusion of these warning signs the sudden destruction of the day of the Lord will begin. Birth pangs. And this beginning has destruction described by 1 Thessalonians 5:1-3 and is on a scale that mankind has never before seen.

CHAPTER THREE

The Birth Pangs Beginning Phase

This chapter covers the events that mark the horrific birth pangs beginning phase of the day of the Lord. In more common language this is what the beginning of the end times looks like based on an array of scripture. These events can be isolated as occurring at the beginning by establishing that the beginning of the day of the Lord is the beginning of the end times. We know this from a simplistic and literal reading of several scriptures. As previously covered in 1 Thessalonians 5:1-3, Paul specifically tells us that the sudden start of the day of the Lord is birth pangs. As there is no beginning of the end times before birth pangs, then upon this foundation of truth we build.

Jesus tells us in Matthew 24:8 that the events He describes in verse 7 are the beginning. And the word used is the same for birth pangs in 1 Thessalonians 5. The established that birth pangs and the beginning are used interchangeably. Additionally, His description of nations rising to war, as well as famine, pestilences, and earthquakes, broadly check off the destruction wrought by the four horsemen of the apocalypse described by John in Revelation chapter 6 — the beginning chapter in that book of horrific events associated with the end times. And at the end of the chapter, he describes its events as the wrath of God. The literal definition of the day of the Lord.

As such there is no scriptural doubt that what we call the beginning of the end times is the beginning of the day of the Lord. And that there is a devastating beginning phase to it referred to as birth pangs. And upon those secure foundations is this chapter based.

Warfare

There is warfare — great warfare that starts suddenly and appears to be the dreaded World War III mankind has tried so hard to avoid. It is Jesus who leaves this impression by going out of His way to include the full spectrum of government entities going to war within His "nation shall rise against nation, and kingdom against kingdom" warning in Matthew 24:7. Within His description He alerts us to the peaceful condition of the nations' before its launch by telling us the nations must rise when it begins. Paul concurs concerning this peaceful condition telling us in 1 Thessalonians 5:1-3 the great war's beginning will be sudden, indicating the nations are at rest prior to it starting. Paul goes as far as to tell us the nations will embrace a delusion just before the great war begins. They believe they have found Peace — furthering the notion they are quietly settled before it suddenly begins. However, this Peace will not flutter on the wings of angels, but only in the minds of men.

In Revelation 6 the apostle John, writing on the Isle of Patmos in the Aegean Sea, describes this war as the "red horse," loosed by the "second seal," which is unleashed by the hand of Jesus from heaven. And the result of those nations and kingdoms suddenly rising to war is described broadly by John as taking "peace from the earth." That is the "earth" and not a part of it. What else should be expected from a horse of the apocalypse? Then as if to stress how much warfare is happening we are also told the "pale horse," loosed from the unsealing of the "fourth seal," is "to kill with the sword."

How terrible is this great war that launches the day of the Lord? 2 Peter gives us a glimpse. Whereas in 1 Thessalonians 5:1-3 Paul tells us the sudden destruction that starts of the day of the Lord represents its birth pangs beginning, 2 Peter adds a grim detail to that beginning. After repeating Paul's admonition that "the day of the Lord will come as a thief in the night," what he describes can only be nuclear detonations.

> [10] But the day of the Lord will come as a thief in the night;
> in the which the heavens shall pass away with a great
> noise, and the elements shall melt with fervent heat, the
> earth also and the works that are therein shall be burned
> up. 2 Peter 3:10

Once nations begin using nuclear weapons against each other madness and rage overtake reason. The result is an escalating cycle of destruction to subdue one's foe until neither can lift their arms. In the end "all nations" are left devastated. The "full end" spoken of by Jeremiah.

How devastated will all nations be after the birth pangs phase of the day of the Lord? Not only will mankind have to deal with the horrors and devastation of nuclear blasts, but the radioactive aftermath that would follow. Such an environmental calamity would necessarily contaminate the food and water supply of the planet resulting in more deaths than the blasts themselves. Those who survive the blasts would have to exercise great caution in burying the dead for fear of exposure to dangerous elements. This ghoulish condition would result in tremendous "pestilence" spread from hordes of decaying bodies similar to the time of the black plague in Europe — a horror that killed one-third of the population on the continent and was spread by contact between people. And "famine" would be especially severe since large portions of the earth's landmass would experience radioactive dust on its top-soil creating deadly crops. Much of the land that the dust doesn't contaminate would eventually experience radioactive rainfall.

As a result of such devastation, the greatest power vacuum in world history will appear. This explains why it is during the birth pangs beginning phase of the day of the Lord that the Antichrist rises to world power.

This is noted in Revelation 6 where upon the undoing of the first seal he is spotted riding the "white horse conquering and to conquer." Such conquest eventually puts him in a position to confirm the agreement previously initiated by all nations that are now the conquered. Power transfers from all nations to the Antichrist during and as a result of birth pangs.

In the Olivet Discourse, the list of judgments against the nations is described by Jesus in Matthew 24:7: wars, "pestilences, famines and earthquakes." All of these are also checked off by John in Revelation 6. The only difference is that John uses an entire chapter to describe them and therefore provides much more detail. This matching of events is no coincidence. Both Jesus and John are describing the birth pangs beginning phase of the day of the Lord.

The Book of Revelation has a simple structure. Seven seals unleash all end-time judgments. Of those seven seals the first six unfold within chapter 6. The final "seventh seal" does not get opened until two chapters later in chapter 8. It is completely separate from the first six. The first six seals open in chapter 6 are birth pangs. It is that seventh seal unleashes the seven-year tribulation consisting of fourteen judgments: the seven trumpet judgments followed by the seven bowl judgments. Birth pangs birth the seven years. What we call the end times is the day of the Lord. It has a beginning phase called birth pangs which birth the seven years. It is that simple.

So the first six seals in Revelation 6 represent the unleashing of the birth pangs beginning of the day of the Lord. Thereafter the seven-year tribulation unfolds from the massive seventh seal and the fourteen judgments flowing from it. Although the birth pangs beginning phase is separate from the seven-year tribulation, both fall within the broader time frame of the day of the Lord. That is why the Antichrist is first seen in Revelation 6 riding the white horse. On it, we are told he went out conquering and to conquer. He takes control during the tumultuous and devastatingly destructive birth pangs beginning phase. That white horse of the apocalypse is unleashed by the first seal. His rise on the white horse during birth pangs places him in position to later confirm the agreement all nations previously initiated. That is why it is only after he has risen during birth pangs that he shall confirm the covenant with many, (initiated by all nations) birthing the seven-year tribulation. Daniel's 70th week is born out of birth pangs. Birth pangs birth Daniel's final week of years. It is that simple.

The prophet Isaiah in chapter 13 speaks of birth pangs as well with the phrase: "They will be in pain as a woman in childbirth." He tells us it comes as "destruction from the Almighty." That it is "the day of His fierce anger." And where does the Lord fulfill "His fierce anger" against all nations? Joel 3 tells us they are brought into the Valley of Jehoshaphat, the theatre of God's judgment against all nations during the birth pangs beginning of the end times. Joel also uses the term later in the chapter for the Battle of Armageddon at the end of the end times. As mentioned previously the phrase is a book-end of end-time judgments against all nations — marking both the opening and closing of great wars which devastate them.

It is easy to see how this warfare will fulfill Albert Einstein's famous words: "I know not with what weapons World War III will be fought, but World War IV will be fought with sticks and stones." Birth pangs sound a lot like Einstein's World War III. It is only part of the horrid birthing process ultimately leading to the seven-year tribulation.

More Sorrows

Then in rapid succession John the Revelator tells of the "black horse" and "pale horse" being loosened bringing pestilence and famine to a world already wracked by warfare more deadly than any before matching Jesus' admonitions in Matthew 24:7 of famine and pestilence in the beginning of sorrows — birth pangs. Is radioactive fallout contaminating most of the world's food supply causing both plagues? Or do the nations of the world add the horror of biological warfare to the plight of each other? The rider of the pale horse speaks of "the beasts of the earth" plaguing mankind. A likely reference to biological agents of death and not lions, tigers, and bears. Do the multitude of rotting corpses of those killed by sudden destruction, resting on radioactive landscapes and unable to be buried, unleash uncontrollable plagues? That rider of the black horse of the apocalypse loosened from the third seal also holds a pair of scales in his grisly hand. As he does a voice not his speaks of the scarcity of food and that it is very expensive. Famine. As all of this is occurring those still alive can feel the earth moving under their feet.

Great earthquakes are occurring in "divers places" (all over) on the earth according to Luke's rendition of the Olivet Discourse (Luke 21). The Greek word "megas" is used for great to stress the uniquely powerful nature of them. So powerful is a "mega" earthquake that the United States Geological Survey, the world's premier organization for tracking earthquake activity states that never have they recorded a single mega earthquake since sensing devices started being placed across the globe around the year 1900. They define mega as 10.0 or higher on the Richter scale. According to Luke, these are occurring all over the earth. Revelation 6 focuses on one particularly great earthquake that shakes the entire world. John says so great is this earthquake that "every mountain and island was moved out of its place." And why are there so many great earthquakes suddenly beginning all over the earth moving "every mountain and island ... out of its place?" It may be for two reasons.

Earthquakes

When the grim reaper of nuclear war looms the matter of national survival takes center stage. As such nations fearing an attack consider a first-strike option against their foe. It is a choice between the quick and the dead. The one who strikes first has the best chance of survival. The slow one can lose much of their nuclear arsenal, suddenly finding themselves at the mercy of a merciless foe. As a result, this mentality tends to produce a hair-trigger finger on the nuclear button at times of international stress. This can certainly lead to the sudden destruction Paul describes in the birth-pangs opening scene of the end times. One place the quick will seek to use their salves of death is in the depths of the oceans where enemy nuclear submarines lurk. Seeking to destroy them before they can release their deadly offspring.

Is it nuclear detonations triggering major fault lines on the earth that Luke 21 is describing? Luke adds the detail of the "sea and waves roaring." Would this condition result from great earthquakes erupting on the sea floor as nations send nuclear bombs into the depths of the oceans to destroy submarines nesting there? Or is it something else impacting the earth causing these great earthquakes and tidal disruptions? As survivors gaze upward into the cosmos the frightening answer will appear before their stricken eyes.

CHAPTER FOUR

Cosmic Terror

As the Lord's wrath unfolds across a world wracked by the worst wars, famines, pestilences and great earthquakes in its history, a dark celestial wild card appears in space. It is the "sixth seal." The last of the birth pangs seals to open. This leaves only the "seventh seal" opened two chapters later which unleashes the seven trumpet judgments followed by the seven bowl judgments — the seven-year tribulation. These horrific birth pangs are only the beginning of the end times.

> [12] I looked when He opened the sixth seal, and behold,
> there was a great earthquake; and the sun became black
> as sackcloth of hair, and the moon became like blood.
> [13] And the stars of heaven fell to the earth, as a fig tree
> drops its late figs when it is shaken by a mighty wind.

The sky is darkened and not only at night. The moon is red. The sky is falling with a multitude of objects raining down like figs from a tree when it is "shaken by a mighty wind." There must be many and they have the appearance of falling stars. John's mysterious description flows into more mystery as objects rain down upon the earth. And the sky is disappearing.

[14] Then the sky receded as a scroll when it is rolled up,
and every mountain and island was moved out of its place.

The prophet Amos adds to the mystery.

[9]"And it shall come to pass in that day," says the Lord GOD,
"That I will make the sun go down at noon,
And I will darken the earth in broad daylight; Amos 8:9

A sight never before seen by men unfolds before their eyes. The day sky begins to slowly disappear. Something is blocking light from reaching the earth at the same time great spiritual darkness engulfs the planet. It dominates the heavens. Its gravitational pull contorts the earth like a flimsy reed in the wind moving "every mountain and island … out of its place." And all men regardless of rank react the same.

[15] And the kings of the earth, the great men, the rich men,
the commanders, the mighty men, every slave and every
free man, hid themselves in the caves and in the rocks of
the mountains,

[16] and said to the mountains and rocks, "Fall on us and
hide us from the face of Him who sits on the throne and
from the wrath of the Lamb!

Be ye a king or be ye a slave all men seek the shelter of the cave. Mankind is forced into becoming a modern troglodyte. And the inherent wickedness of men tells them who is behind this wrath. They try to hide from He who has no beginning. But they cannot. Because His wrath has come.

[17] For the great day of His wrath has come, and who is able
to stand?" Revelation 6:12-17

By definition, the wrath of God is the day of the Lord. And these six seal judgments are simply its opening scene. These terrible events are nothing more than end-time birth pangs. The beginning phase of the day of the Lord. Soon to be followed by the seven-year tribulation unleashed by the powerful seventh seal. As for the sixth seal and its strange descriptions one candidate for its fulfillment appears to stand out.

Asteroid or Comet

From the description of these prophecies it would appear the best candidate capable of fulfilling them would be a very large asteroid or comet passing very close to the earth. As its hulking mass slowly moves between the sun and the earth, a dark shadow would cover the sky as though it were being rolled up like a scroll. It would also produce something else.

Falling Stars

Asteroids are not lone travelers through the vastness of space. They travel with a great company of friends called "debris clouds." These debris clouds consist of countless meteorites and meteors of various sizes. As a result, a large asteroid that passes close enough to Earth to wreak gravitational havoc on mountains and islands would also hurl down to the Earth's surface raining clouds of "falling stars" the like of which has never before been seen. Millions upon millions would plunge in fiery descent through the atmosphere creating an appearance like the stars of heaven fell to the earth, "as a fig tree drops its late figs when it is shaken by a mighty wind." And naturally, people would seek protection. Since the speeding hot rocks would easily cut through the typical rooftop like a hot knife through butter few would be safe. But those within rock enclaves — caves — would be safe. And the whole affair would usher in the fearful sights and great signs from heaven Luke 21 speaks of during birth pangs, as well as the sea and waves roaring completing the beginning phase of the day of the Lord — the end times.

Scripture is very clear that after this horrific birth pangs phase is finished the final seven years of the Lord's redemptive plan for man begins. Daniel's 70th week is popularly called the seven-year tribulation. Birth pangs announce the impending birth of the 70th week. Knowing that the tribulation period lasts seven years raises the most obvious question. How long do birth pangs last?

The Year of Recompense

Anchors in Bible prophecy are welcomed and often are found in specific statements or phrases used by the prophets that allow us to connect prophecies. And one such anchor is found in Isaiah 34. This should sound familiar.

> 4All the host of heaven shall be dissolved,
> And the heavens shall be rolled up like a scroll;
> All their host shall fall down
> As the leaf falls from the vine,
> And as fruit falling from a fig tree. Isaiah 34:4

Isaiah is describing the same event as John's sixth seal in Revelation 6. And we know Revelation 6 represents the birth pangs beginning. So we can understand that Isaiah 34 must also be describing events that will take place during birth pangs. He also mentions the indignation of the Lord is against all nations. The same all nations other prophets assure us are dealt a full end during birth pangs. And then we are told this.

> For it is the day of the LORD's vengeance,
> The year of recompense for the controversy of Zion.
> Isaiah 34:8

The word for "recompense" is the Hebrew noun "shilluwm" which essentially means retribution. The word for "controversy" is the Hebrew noun "riyb" which means a dispute, strife, controversy, or quarrel. But not warfare. And Zion is another way of saying Jerusalem. Now the picture forms.

Just as the other prophets have indicated there is a controversy, dispute, or quarreling involving Israeli land before birth pangs begin. But no mention of warfare. In fact, from Joel, we know it is the division of land that launches the day of the Lord. And we know from a multitude of prophets that the division takes place by a Peace agreement. And according to Joel and Jeremiah, it is initiated by all nations — the United Nations — the covenant with many Daniel speaks of. Isaiah is adding the detail that the Israeli capital of Jerusalem is impacted during birth pangs. This makes sense since it has long been the goal of the United Nations (all nations) to remove East Jerusalem from Israeli control and give it to the Palestinians. Not only do these verses add that detail, but they may also indicate how long birth pangs last.

The word "year" in the verse is the Hebrew feminine noun "sana" meaning a literal year or simply a division of time. The prophet's words may be indicating this birth pangs beginning phase is a separate prophetic division of time from the seven-year tribulation. And, of course, we already know birth pangs birth the seven-years and are separate from it coming before it. But it is also possible he is telling us birth pangs will last one literal year.

After cosmic terrors torment the planet sewing fear in the hearts of men, and causing them to scurry for safety, the skies across the earth have yet another dark message to deliver upon the punished and battered world. The accumulation of fires across the globe from the great war leaves an indelible mark on the atmosphere of the planet.

A Day of Clouds and Thick Darkness

Sometime after rocks from space speed through the atmosphere in their fiery decent, and radioactive fire and steel rain down from the wars of men, in the sky above will float a sheath of darkness unlike anything ever before seen. Like a great cloak covering the planet dark clouds blanket a world convulsing in the accumulation of sin, hiding its shame and nakedness from the rest of the universe. Joel speaks of this darkness.

> For the day of the Lord is coming,
> For it is at hand:
> A day of darkness and gloominess,
> A day of clouds and thick darkness, Joel 2:1-2

The impact of a heavenly body passing so close to the earth, sending countless streaming balls of fire through the atmosphere, combined with nuclear detonations and their endless fires, will result in clouds of darkness blossoming in the skies of the world. The massively powerful bombs detonating across the earth's surface will send unthinkable amounts of dirt, smoke, ash and debris into the atmosphere. The effects will be staggering on the planet. The prophet Zephaniah places it in context.

> [14] The great day of the LORD is near; It is near and hastens quickly.
> The noise of the day of the LORD is bitter; There the mighty men shall cry out. That day is a day of wrath, a day of trouble and distress, a day of wasteness and desolation, <u>a day of darkness and gloominess, a day of clouds and thick darkness</u>... Zephaniah 1:14

Human senses are intense during times of great stress. And during the day of the Lord, the sense of hearing will be overwhelmed by the noise of nuclear blasts. Incomparable explosions never before heard by men on the earth. Zephaniah tells us: "The noise of the day of the Lord is bitter." This is similar to what we read in 2 Peter 3 "in the which the heavens shall pass away with a great noise." The human sense of seeing will also be overpowered. Transformed into a portal of horror absorbing the sight of vast "wasteness and desolation" where once there had been life and order.

Reference points allowing people to identify their location disappear, turning confused hordes into wandering nomads seeking the familiar. In the aftermath of nuclear devastation, there will be great fires.

> [1]Blow ye the trumpet in Zion, and sound an alarm in my holy mountain: let all the inhabitants of the land tremble: for the day of the Lord cometh, for it is nigh at hand;
>
> [2]A day of darkness and of gloominess, a day of clouds and of thick darkness, as the morning spread upon the mountains: a great people and a strong; there hath not been ever the like, neither shall be any more after it, even to the years of many generations.
>
> [3]A fire devoureth before them; and behind them a flame burneth: the land is as the garden of Eden before them, and behind them a desolate wilderness; yea, and nothing shall escape them. Joel 2:1-3 & 10-11

After a "fire" has had its way of devouring what once was, it leaves behind a simple "flame" as its calling card. What had been like the "Garden of Eden before" the fire came is transformed into "desolate wilderness" thereafter. "Nothing shall escape." The massive fires raging across the tormented world add countless millions of tons of ash and soot into the atmosphere compounding the darkness. An excerpt from an article in *The Atomic Scientist* captures the elemental impact nuclear conflict would have on the atmosphere.

Nuclear Winter

In a 2012 article published in "The Atomic Scientist," authors A. Robock and O.B. Toon, suggest that dense smoke from a nuclear war would block sunlight and plunge the world into darkness. Without warmth and sunlight for photosynthesis, plant life would die triggering mass starvation up the food chain. The authors

further speculate even small-scale use of nuclear war-
heads could deplete the ozone layer, shorten the growing season, increase temperature and hasten the effects
of global warming. http://education.seattlepi.com/
nuclear-bombs-affect-environment-6173.html

In the aftermath of nuclear detonations there would not only be an
enormous volume of dust and particles blasted into the atmosphere from the
initial explosions, but the resulting fires from those blasts would add unmea-
surable amounts of smoke, soot and ash as well. Such content injected into
the atmosphere would block light from all celestial bodies — the sun, moon
and stars from reaching the Earth. And that is an important distinction.

The distinction is between the heavenly warning sign coming before
the day of the Lord launches, and the heavenly condition during the day
of the Lord. This distinction is a source of great confusion. It is easy to
mistakenly blend the two together.

The heavenly warning sign that the end times are about to begin is:
"The sun shall be turned into darkness, and the moon into blood." The
stars are not included because this scripture refers to a heavenly sign and
not a condition of the atmosphere impacting the visibility of all heavenly
bodies. That is why the heavenly descriptions during the day of the Lord
include not only the sun and the moon but also the stars. Because all are
impacted by the condition of the atmosphere. An event in 2010 provided a
brief look at what the "day of clouds and of thick darkness" might be like
during the day of the Lord.

In that year a volcano in Iceland blew its top spewing 250 million
cubic meters of ejected ash, dust, and cinders into the atmosphere. The
nation most impacted by the premortal release was Great Britain. Having
risen to a height of 30,000 feet, the massive plume created by the billowing
mammoth, created a blanket so thick over the heavens of Britain that air
travel in and out of the country had to be suspended. The impact of the
prehistoric giant soon engulfed the European continent.

That event is a brief foretaste of a bitter cup that one day will be served across a fallen world. The darkness of that time is a monumental event spoken of by other prophets as well.

> "For the day is near, Even the day of the LORD is near; <u>It will be a day of clouds</u>, A time of doom for the nations… Ezekiel 30:3

And yet another.

> Alas, you who are longing for the day of the LORD, For what purpose will the day of the LORD be to you? <u>It will be darkness and not light;</u> As when a man flees from a lion And a bear meets him, Or goes home, leans his hand against the wall And a snake bites him. <u>Will not the day of the LORD be darkness instead of light, Even gloom with no brightness in it?</u> Amos 5:18-20

And again Joel…

> [10]The earth shall quake before them; the heavens shall tremble: <u>the sun and the moon shall be dark, and the stars shall withdraw their shining:</u>
>
> [11]And the Lord shall utter his voice before his army: for his camp is very great: for he is strong that executeth his word: for <u>the day of the Lord</u> is great and very terrible; and who can abide it? Joel 2:10-11

And Isaiah…

> [9] Behold, the day of the LORD cometh, cruel both with wrath and fierce anger, to lay the land desolate: and he shall destroy the sinners thereof out of it.

> ¹⁰ <u>For the stars of heaven and the constellations thereof</u>
> <u>shall not give their light: the sun shall be darkened in his</u>
> <u>going forth, and the moon shall not cause her light to</u>
> <u>shine.</u> Isaiah 13:9-10

However, before darkness overwhelms the skies above the earth there must be a period of respite. This is because scripture is clear that some form of celestial terror will sew fear in the hearts of men when the end times begin. The unwelcomed visitor from space will wreak havoc during the birth pangs beginning of the day of the Lord as noted by its appearance in Revelation 6 — birth pangs. And all scripture noting the darkening of the atmosphere does not specify its unfolding at the beginning. Only sometime during the day of the Lord. If it unfolded immediately at the beginning — birth pangs — then it would be difficult for the prophetic details of the cosmic terror to unfold as foretold.

In this cosmic, terror, we are told: Then the sky receded as a scroll when it is rolled up. The sky must be able to be seen for men to gaze upon its being rolled up like a scroll. Otherwise, how can the prophecy of the prophet Amos be fulfilled wherein the Lord says "I will make the sun go down at noon, And I will darken the earth in broad daylight?" If daylight is blocked then men could not see this unfold. Yet they will. So it would appear that the cosmic terror happens immediately upon birth pangs launching. Whereas the condition of the atmosphere must develop thereafter for both to unfold according to the prophets.

At the Conclusion of Birth Pangs

When the four horsemen of the Apocalypse and the sixth seal with its cosmic terror finally come to an end, the birth pangs beginning phase of the end times are over. The specific birth pangs that launch the end times. Not the general birth pangs that have been building over time. It is the most destructive time in human history except for the flood. Having been brought into the Valley of Jehoshaphat, the place of God's judgment, all nations reach their full end as described by Jeremiah. They are devastated and now ripe for the taking. Common sense says that birth pangs birth something. And the offspring birthed here is the seven-year tribulation. But something else comes out of the ashes of birth pangs and the full end of all nations. A leader who is the first to rule the earth. And he is the worst man that will ever walk its surface. He has many names. But the most notable of them is the Antichrist.

CHAPTER FIVE

The Antichrist and his Kingdom

Within the first verses of Revelation 13, there is a mysterious beast described in terms that are both strange and fearsome. It is a twisted and freakish entity better suited for the winding and fiery caverns of hell than the earth. It is a beast the like of which has never before been seen until it rises from the sea of politics, with the help of the dragon, its blasphemies going before it in a plague of sin and death across the entire earth. Understanding this dark creature is to understand the essence of the Antichrist and the beast kingdom. It is a kingdom that has three distinct parts: "Heads, horns," and animal-like features. And each of these characteristics symbolizes an element of this dark empire.

> Then I stood on the sand of the sea. And I saw a beast rising up out of the sea, having seven heads and ten horns, and on his horns ten crowns, and on his heads a blasphemous name. [2] Now the beast which I saw was like a leopard, his feet were like the feet of a bear, and his mouth like the mouth of a lion. The dragon gave him his power, his throne, and great authority. Revelation 13

Certain prophecy scriptures explain this strange beast and they are presented in the form of riddles. Each is a mystery. And this is done with purpose. Only the correct answer will resolve these mysterious verses. Each of those strange descriptions of the beast kingdom can only be correctly understood by this approach. When the correct answer is found to one riddle, it will fit within and not conflict with the others. In this way is it possible to know that the correct answers have been found in explaining the strange anatomy of the beast kingdom.

The Sixth King...the Antichrist

First, we will look at the "seven heads." And within those verses, we discover that the Beast Kingdom will have no more than seven kings and that the Antichrist will be both the sixth and eighth king. This sounds confusing but soon the answer to this riddle becomes clear. With clarity, it will inform us that the Beast Kingdom will exist in its Biblical form for about 100 years before the Antichrist takes the throne. And by doing something of a reverse-engineering of current events, we will see that he must now be very close to taking the throne. But first, consider the following passage that is presented in the form of a riddle. Then we will resolve it and gain a critical insight.

> [8] The beast that you saw was, and is not, and will ascend out of the bottomless pit and go to perdition. And those who dwell on the earth will marvel, whose names are not written in the Book of Life from the foundation of the world, when they see the beast that was, and is not, and yet is. Revelation 17

How can the Antichrist be the "beast that was, and is not, and yet is?" We are literally being told he exists, then does not exist, and then does exist. By itself, this passage is a mystery dangling in the mind of man. Here is the next mystery passage and riddle.

> [9] "Here is the mind which has wisdom: The <u>seven heads</u> are seven mountains on which the woman sits. [10] There are also <u>seven kings</u>. Five have fallen, one is, and the other has not yet come. And when he comes, he must continue a short time. [11] <u>The beast that was, and is not, is himself also the eighth, and is of the seven</u>, and is going to perdition. Revelation 17

John tells us the "seven heads" are "seven mountains" as well as "seven kings" on which the "woman sits." They support her. She is the Mother of Harlots who is mentioned several verses earlier. Here is the riddle. Although within this succession of rulers, there are no more than seven kings, and the beast (Antichrist) is one "of the seven," he is "also the eighth." How can he be the eighth when there are no more than seven of which he is one? It seems impossible. Here is the last mysterious passage.

> [3] And I saw one of his <u>heads</u> as if it had been mortally wounded, and his deadly wound was healed. And all the world marveled and followed the beast. Revelation 13

Prior to this verse, we are also told about a beast rising up out of the sea having seven heads and other strange appendages. Just as we saw in Revelation 17. This scripture then directly tells us one of the beast's seven heads suffers a "deadly wound" which then was "healed." The mystery is what is meant by one of his heads? How can a person — the Antichrist — have seven heads. How strange. However, each of these three passages has the key to understanding the other. Here is their resolution.

We know from Revelation 17:9-11 that the seven heads are not just mountains, but also a succession of kings. We are told about the fate of the first five kings, then one that is, another to come, and then the eighth. So in Revelation 13 when we are told one of his heads suffers a mortal wound, it is referring back to one of those seven kings suffering the mortal wound. Because these kings are depicted as the heads. But we are also told the wound will be healed and he will return from the dead in a kind of resurrection. This makes one of the seven kings the beast that was, and is not, and yet is. Before suffering the deadly wound he was, after the deadly wound, he is not, and after it is healed he yet is. Since we are told the Antichrist is the eighth king he must also be the sixth king to solve the riddles. It must be the Antichrist — the sixth king — who suffers the deadly wound. Then he is followed by the seventh king who we are told lasts a short time. When the Antichrist comes back to life he reassumes the throne as the eighth king displacing the seventh. We are told the seventh king lasts only a short time because the Antichrist apparently does not stay dead for long. Probably three days mimicking the resurrection of Christ. Even though there are only seven kings Antichrist is the eighth because he is both the sixth and also the eighth king. Resolved. Now consider the story in Daniel 11 about a vile king who relays the same sequence of events.

The Story of the Vile King

A story is told in Daniel 11 of a "vile" leader. How bad is this man? Although the word vile is found 13 times in the Bible, this leader has the distinction of being the only person individually labeled by a prophet as such. And for good reason. He replaces a leader who held power for only a "few days." Oddly, the brief king apparently relinquishes his crown in neither "anger or in battle." How unusual. Why would anyone strong enough to reach the throne give it up without a fight? By now you should suspect that the Antichrist is involved. Because wherever he appears so does a gnarled and perverse story that requires unraveling. And the process of unraveling this story takes us to the verse just before the brief leader appears. It describes the fate of the king just before him.

> ¹⁹ Then he shall turn his face toward the fortress of his own land; but he shall stumble and <u>fall</u>, and not be found.

This king shall "fall." The Hebrew verb for fall is "naphal" which occasionally means to fall "of violent death" according to Strong's Concordance. A good example of this usage is found in Leviticus 26:7. "You will chase your enemies, and they shall <u>fall</u> by the sword before you." Now consider the leader who replaces him after his fall.

> [20] "There shall arise in his place one who imposes taxes on the glorious kingdom; but within <u>a few days</u> he shall be destroyed, but <u>not in anger or in battle</u>.

The key point is not that he "imposes taxes." But that "within a <u>few days</u> he shall be destroyed, but not in anger or in battle." He only remains in power for a few days and is not removed in anger or in battle. Now consider the next person who takes over after this leader is gone.

> [21] And in his place shall arise a <u>vile person</u>, to whom they will not give the honor of royalty; but he shall come in peaceably, and seize the kingdom by intrigue.

It is generally accepted that the "vile person" is the Antichrist. This conclusion becomes increasingly obvious as his story continues until the end of chapter 11. We are told he replaces the king who only lasts a few days. Now consider the flow of events.

A king shall fall possibly by the sword. The leader that replaces him stays only a few days and is not removed in anger or in battle. Then the vile person — the Antichrist — replaces him. This is the same flow of events we saw in the resolution of the riddles of Revelation 13 & 17 explaining the beast that was, and is not, and yet is. But there is more.

A detail given in Revelation 17 seems to explain why Daniel initially refers to the Antichrist as a king and then his reference to him changes to the vile person when he comes back to life after suffering the deadly wound. And this detail is as informative as it is disturbing.

The beast that you saw was, and is not, <u>and will ascend out of the bottomless pit</u> and go to perdition. Revelation 17:8

Going back to Revelation 17 and the description of the Antichrist we are told that what awakens within the body of the Antichrist after suffering the "deadly wound… will ascend out of the bottomless pit." It is not human. It comes from "out of the bottomless pit" and possesses him. This bottomless pit is the place God cast the angels who sinned… delivering them into chains of darkness, to be reserved for judgment according to 2 Peter 2. But in Revelation 9 its prisoners are released back to the earth in a scene of smoke so great that the sun and the air are darkened because of the smoke of the pit. More darkness added to the earth's darkest time.

The discovery that the Antichrist is the sixth king within the Beast kingdom is one of the most informative pieces of prophetic information in recent years. It tells us that the Beast kingdom existed in its Biblical form for only about 100 years or so before the Antichrist will rise to its throne. But no doubt elements of it likely evolved over the course of centuries. But its evolution into its very orderly Biblical form indicates it likely came into its kingdom status sometime around the year 1900. Coincidentally, around the time that the Federal Reserve was established. An entity that empowered a concentration of wealth and power beyond the dreams of King Solomon. Is this why so many industries have evolved into purveyors of darkness? One can only speculate. Now let's continue unraveling the Beast Kingdom.

The Lion, Leopard, and the Bear

In further dissecting the strange creature from the sea we find that the beast has friends. Better to say, accomplices. And, of course, they too are presented in mystery form. Mysteries abound when it comes to the beast kingdom. In addition to the seven heads and ten horns, the beast kingdom possesses the characteristics of a lion, leopard, and bear. Here is their description in Revelation 13

> ² Now the beast which I saw was like a leopard, his feet were like the feet of a bear, and his mouth like the mouth of a lion. The dragon gave him his power, his throne, and great authority. Revelation 13:2

Who else but the dragon would be behind such a distorted beast? It takes the prophet Daniel to provide critical clues as to what these animals represent. And once that is understood then speculation as to who they are becomes possible. Consider the full descriptions of these beasts given by Daniel.

> ² Daniel spoke, saying, "I saw in my vision by night, and behold, the four winds of heaven were stirring up the Great Sea. ³ And four great beasts came up from the sea, each different from the other. ⁴ The first was like **a lion, and had eagle's wings**. I watched till its wings were plucked off; and it was lifted up from the earth and made to stand on two feet like a man, and a man's heart was given to it.
>
> ⁵ "And suddenly another beast, a second, like **a bear**. It was raised up on one side, and had three ribs in its mouth between its teeth. And they said thus to it: 'Arise, devour much flesh!'
>
> ⁶ "After this I looked, and there was another, like **a leopard**, which had on its back four wings of a bird. The beast also had four heads, and dominion was given to it. Daniel 7:2-6

There are "four great beasts." The fourth is the horrid Antichrist kingdom. But it is the first three we are focused on. The debate concerning those first three the lion, leopard and bear, centers on whether they are ancient kingdoms from the past, or if they will be contemporary major allies of the Antichrist. And the issue can be easily resolved thanks to Daniel.

Those thinking they are kingdoms of the past associate these beasts with the kingdoms presented in a prophecy found in Daniel 2. As such they say the lion, leopard and bear represent the ancient kingdoms of Babylon, Media-Persia and Greece. In Daniel 2 those ancient kingdoms are presented as anatomical parts of a statue that the king Nebuchadnezzar saw in a dream. Babylon, for example, is its head. Therefore, according to this perspective, their relevance to future events is limited. However, the following passage in Daniel 7 disputes that perspective.

> [11] "I watched then because of the sound of the pompous words which the horn was speaking; I watched till the beast was slain, and its body destroyed and given to the burning flame. [12] As for the rest of the beasts, they had their dominion taken away, yet their lives were prolonged for a season and a time. Daniel 7:11-12

Daniel begins by describing the fate of the Antichrist — the "fourth beast" — noting that the twisted wreckage of this person and his kingdom finally come to a fiery end. Then in the same breath the ultimate fate of the rest of the "beasts" is described. Telling us that as the ferocious Antichrist is being relegated to eternal fire, the other three beasts face a different fate. Their dominion is taken away ruling out the possibility they are faint shadows of a distant past. They are contemporary to the Antichrist kingdom being punished concurrent with him having their "dominion taken away" at the time he is thrust into the fire. As the beast kingdom is dissolved into the ash heap of history the lives of the lion, leopard, and bear continue without dominion, but are now limited to "a season and a time." They are allowed to outlive the Antichrist for a short time. Since the lion, leopard and bear are clearly separate powers from the Antichrist kingdom, but aligned with it and facing a similar fate, this description of the final disposition of all four beasts makes it clear that the lion, leopard, and bear are major allied nations of the dark Antichrist kingdom. Similar to what Italy and Japan represented to the odious Nazi regime of the 1930s and 40s.

But sometimes wrong teachings die a stubborn death. And the notion that the lion, leopard, and bear are from the ancient past is one of them. As mentioned earlier that theory has those three beasts as ancient Babylon, Media-Persia, and Greece. However, consider that Daniel 8 rules out ancient Media-Persia and Greece from being any part of these beasts.

> ²⁰ The <u>ram</u> which you saw, having the two horns— they are the kings of Media and Persia. ²¹ And the male <u>goat</u> is the kingdom of Greece. The large horn that is between its eyes is the first king. Daniel 8:20-21

In Daniel 8 we are told that the ancient kingdoms of Media/Persia and Greece have specific animal symbolism associated with them. The "ram" for Media/Persia and the "goat" for Greece. This rules out the possibility that either can be the lion, leopard, or bear in the previous chapter. Otherwise, it is necessary to believe the Holy Spirit used one set of animal depictions in chapter 7 and then changed them in chapter 8 when speaking about the same kingdoms. And that should be a bridge too far to cross by any who respect the consistency of God.

All of this makes it very probable that these three beasts in chapter 7 are contemporary major allies of the Antichrist kingdom. Now the question arises as to which nations they refer to at the time this prophecy will be fulfilled. Since the nations are not specifically identified in the way Daniel 8 identifies ancient Media-Persia and Greece, then we are relegated to logical speculation. Speculation and not certainty. One reason they may not be specifically identified is because these nation-states did not exist at the time the prophecy was given. Therefore, animal symbolism was used so they could later be identified when their time arrived.

Bible prophecy is informative. And for the information concerning these three beasts to be informative the animal depictions used should have meaning in the present day. Since these allies are noted in the prophecies multiple times we should believe they will be <u>major</u> allies. So the nations they depict should have notable standing and power relative to the vast array of nations on the earth today. If they were insignificant allies then they would not warrant so much Biblical attention. And this alone eliminates many candidate nations.

In the modern age, certain animals are used to depict various nations. The roar of the British lion was heard around the world at one time. It was even said that the sun never set on its territory. Although their empire is now history the use of the lion to depict Great Britain is not. During the cold war, there was a Time magazine cover that pitted the bear against the eagle. The bear, of course, was Russia and the eagle the United States. Those animals were used for the two countries because they are generally accepted in the current day as symbolic of both. As for the leopard that one is not clear. Some speculate it is Germany. But the jury is out as that is not its national animal.

Accordingly, if the animal symbolism used by Daniel is meant to identify these major nations allied with the Antichrist at the time his ungodly kingdom is on earth, then at least the lion and the bear appear to be identifiable. Additionally, since the lion has eagle's wings that are plucked off then it would appear the United States is also mentioned. And one solid geopolitical fact in the modern age is that the United States and Great Britain are the closest of allies. So the lion having eagle wings may very well indicate the closeness of both nations. Based on this speculation here is what we gleam.

Speculation

Great Britain aligns with the savage Antichrist kingdom. At the time they do so, the United States is still firmly attached to the old alliance with them. This would appear to be the case because at the time the lion joins with the Antichrist the eagle's wings are still attached. But then we are told: I watched till its wings were plucked off. Perhaps a leader in the U.S. led by the Lord will end the United States-Britain alliance at that point. If so then the United States would also be breaking away from the Antichrist kingdom. Some speculate the eagle's wings breaking off from the lion is symbolic of the American Revolutionary war. Wherein the fledgling American colonies broke away from the mother country. But that is unlikely since scripture describes the condition of these Antichrist allies at the time they partner with him and not some time frame in their past. And the eagle's wings are with Britain as the lion enters into the pit of darkness to join the Antichrist. All of this speculation is completely based on the lion representing Great Britain and the eagle's wings representing the United States.

Should this speculation be correct then there are various political realities inferred. The sudden removal of the eagle's wings would seem to indicate that the close alliance between Great Britain and the United States will come to an abrupt halt. But also that the United States may enter into a kind of fortress America-type isolation in an attempt to avoid the far-reaching and powerful tentacles of the Antichrist empire. The other possibility is that the U.S. will go into active opposition against the Antichrist. The fact that the United States is initially alongside Britain in alliance with the Antichrist opens the possibility of a White House initially darkened by a black shadow. But the abrupt removal of the eagle's wings may indicate a freeing of America from this dark grip by God. It also indicates a right-of-center government in charge in the United States. This is because any left-of-center government, currently referred to as "progressive" (an oxymoron term), would likely embrace the Antichrist due to their common anti-God beliefs. But there is another possibility.

After the great destruction of all nations during the birth pangs beginning of the day of the Lord, both the United States and Great Britain having experienced Jeremiah's full end, are incapable of resisting the Antichrist who rides the white horse of Revelation 6 during that time to take over the world. Whereas Great Britain remains under his boot for the duration of the end times, the United States breaks free from his wicked grasp. Possibly because of the hundreds of millions of firearms spread out across the vast North American continent. This may all infer hope for the eagle. It is all speculative as there are no cross-referencing scriptures relating to the lion and the eagle to gain more context.

The Ten Horns

The bazaar beast from the sea, rising up with seven heads and ten horns, is contorted with the images of a lion, leopard, and a bear. It is a foul thing filled with blasphemies that will take the lives and souls of countless millions. The seven heads are a succession of kings leading up to the Antichrist. He being the sixth and the eighth due to suffering the deadly wound. The lion, leopard and bear are his loathsome allies joining him in blood lust. But this beast also has ten horns. And as with everything associated with it, the description of the ten horns is both strange and contradictory.

> [12] "The ten horns which you saw are ten kings who have received <u>no kingdom as yet</u>, but they receive authority for one hour as kings with the beast. [13] These are of one mind, and they will give their power and authority to the beast. Revelation 17

They are kings. But they have "no kingdom." "Yet." But they are kings. How can they be kings before they receive their kingdom? And after receiving authority for "one hour as kings" — not a kingdom for one hour but only authority for one hour as kings — and being "of one mind," they return their momentary power to the beast. These are very strange kings indeed! They have no real power of their own. And no kingdom. At least not yet which means they will eventually have their kingdom. But in a direct statement of scripture, we are being told that at the point in time in which they exalt the Antichrist to power, they do not have a kingdom. To understand these odd kings it takes a little noticed scripture found in the Book of Isaiah. In it, the prophet repeats words that the Antichrist will one day say. On their own, these words make little sense.

> ⁸ For he says, 'Are not my princes altogether kings?
> Isaiah 10:8

The Hebrew word for "princes" is the masculine noun "sar" used to identify various types of leaders. In the Old Testament, it is used 208 times for prince, 130 times for captain, 33 times for chief, and 33 times for ruler. So these could be literal princes or simply notable leaders.

Another key in the verse is "he." It is the Antichrist. Seven verses earlier he references the "Assyrian the rod of My anger." (KJV) The Lord's anger. And we know from Micah 5:1-6 that the Assyrian is the Antichrist because in the beginning of those verses "Bethlehem Ephratah" is identified as where this man Jesus will be born. Then this in verse 4:

> ···And this man (Jesus from Bethlehem) shall be the peace,
> when the Assyrian shall come into our land: and when he
> shall tread in our palaces, then shall we raise against him
> seven shepherds, and eight principal men. Micah 5:4

This action of the Assyrian has never taken place. It is yet future. And when it does happen it will be Jesus who will deal with him. This is an end-time event with the Antichrist simply being called by one of his many names found throughout scripture. There is also Isaiah 31:4-9. Within those verses, the Assyrian is being dealt with by Jesus when the Lord comes back in the second coming. "Then the Assyrian shall fall by a sword not of man, and a sword not of mankind shall devour him." Isaiah chapters 14 and 10 also speak of the Assyrian as the Antichrist.

These princes that the Antichrist indicates are his kings must also be the same ten kings described in Revelation 17. That is because other than the lion, leopard, and bear, the ten kings are the only kings scripture tells us are intimately associated with him. This would explain why Revelation 17 describes the ten kings as those who have received no kingdom as yet. They must first be princes or powerful leaders who later receive their own kingdoms to rule. At that point, they go from princes to real kings. The prophecy of Revelation 17 uses the title of what these ten despicable princes or leaders will ultimately become. Kings. The prophet John is simply looking backward upon an event yet to happen referring to them by the title of the highest office they will ultimately attain. Kings. Not by the lesser position they will hold along the way. Princes. Consider the example of former president Franklin Roosevelt which is informative to this point.

Before he became President of the United States he was first Governor of New York. But historically no one refers to him as Governor Roosevelt. He is always referred to by the ultimate office he attained. President Roosevelt. That is because we are looking from the present back in time so we refer to him by the ultimate title he attained. However, the truth is that he was governor of a major state before he attained that lofty position. And it was his stepping stone to the presidency. It could be said by New Yorkers of Roosevelt: "Is not my governor also a president." And if a prophet had foretold his rise would he not have called Roosevelt a president even though he was a governor first? But there is something even deeper and darker taking place relative to these ten kings.

One of the main characteristics of the Antichrist is that he seeks to mimic Jesus in as many ways as possible. For example, he will suffer a deadly wound only to come back from the dead in a dark rendition of Jesus' resurrection. He also will have miracles taking place around himself, especially with the help of the false prophet. The false prophet, like John the Baptist for Jesus, declares the Antichrist a god. And the ten kings appear to be another such effort. By making them each a king, (Even before having a kingdom of their own.) when they lift him to his black throne he will have become a king lifted up by other kings. Therefore, he can then claim he is the king of kings in another mimic of Jesus. And this explains these strange kings who have no kingdom at the time they lift up the Antichrist to the throne. And why they are granted authority as kings for only one hour before it is whisked away from them.

Now Revelation 17 again, but in context with the Antichrist telling us 'Are not my princes altogether kings? And keep in mind the word used for princes in Isaiah 10 can also simply mean a notable leader of some kind.

> [12] "The ten horns which you saw are ten kings who have received no kingdom as yet, but they receive authority for one hour as kings with the beast. [13] These are of one mind, and they will give their power and authority to the beast. Revelation 17

Yes, they are called ten kings because they are being referred to by what they will ultimately become. But initially, they must be princes (or notable leaders within a kingdom) just as Isaiah tells us the Antichrist describes them. This explains why these kings initially have no kingdom… yet. That yet is also an important clue. Because it means they will ultimately attain an actual kingdom. But not yet at the point in time wherein they give their support to the Antichrist to establish him. Strangely, at the time they lift up the Antichrist to the beast kingdom throne, we are also told they will be kings for one hour with the beast. The fact that they have to be made kings for one hour at that point also speaks to the fact that they do not even have the title of king until that hour. As well as no actual kingdom. This too speaks to the reality of their lower station as princes initially. More on that in a moment. But all of this speaks to something else.

At the time the Antichrist rises to power, there is no ten-nation or kingdom confederacy yet. (The common teaching today is that he arises out of a ten-nation confederacy based on Daniel 7. More on that later.) Revelation 17 is unambiguous in making it clear that the ten kingdom confederacy comes into existence only after the Antichrist rises from within some kingdom. And since his rise is made possible by these ten princes or notable leaders this supplies ample reason why he will eventually confer upon them literal kingdoms making them actual kings with a kingdom of their own. All of this raises yet another question. Where does the territory come from for these ten princes to receive kingdoms?

That answer is found in Revelation 6. It is there that we see the Antichrist riding the white horse of the Apocalypse going about conquering and to conquer. This conquering is, of course, happening in the opening scene of the end times. Birth pangs. And those conquered countries will need rulers loyal to him. What better group than his ten princes fulfilling Isaiah's statement: For he says, 'Are not my princes altogether kings?' Yes, they will become kings because the Antichrist is the one who makes them so because they are his princes. But only after he rises to power within the strange beast kingdom and conquers.

The direct statement that these ten kings have no kingdom, but they receive authority for one hour as kings with the beast, a very short time, and then give their power and authority right back to the beast, leaves no room for considering them as rulers of an actual kingdom at the time they lift up the beast-Antichrist to his perch of power. With that unambiguous fact as the framework of truth, the prophet Daniel describes a power play as old as history itself involving the ascension of the beast to his dark throne. Daniel starts by setting the stage.

> "Thus he said:
> 'The fourth beast shall be
> A fourth kingdom on earth,
> Which shall be different from all other kingdoms,
> And shall devour the whole earth,
> Trample it and break it in pieces. Daniel 7:23

Of all the kingdoms that have existed upon the earth, the beast kingdom will be "different" from them. And this direct statement of scripture opens the door to a new kind of kingdom — one that has never before existed. More on that in the next chapter. Not only will the beast kingdom "be different from all other kingdoms" that have ever existed on the earth, but it will "devour the whole earth." The ancient words say it will be the whole earth. Leaving little doubt as to the results of the Antichrist riding the white horse going about conquering in Revelation 6. And thus the need for his ten princes to oversee a vast expanse of conquered lands making them actual kings. Now for the power play.

> ²⁴ The ten horns are ten kings
> <u>Who shall arise from this kingdom</u>.
> And another shall rise after them;
> He shall be different from the first ones,
> And shall subdue three kings. Daniel 7:24

In a statement that would otherwise seem strange we hear that the "ten kings arise from this kingdom"… a single kingdom. And obviously, there cannot be ten kings simultaneously ruling a single kingdom. And we know they are not kings in succession to each other since they will simultaneously lift the Antichrist to the throne. This odd statement can only make sense in the context that they initially start off in a lesser position within a kingdom — as princes or leaders — only later fulfilling Isaiah's words of becoming actual kings and fulfilling the yet in Revelation 17. They are simply referred to in the verse by the ultimate positions they will attain. And remember they are granted the title of king prior to attaining a kingdom of their own so the Antichrist can claim to be a king of kings. And since we are also told the Antichrist shall rise after them, we can understand that these princes or leaders have been established within this unusual and different beast kingdom before the ascension of the Antichrist within it. And there is the statement that he is different from them. Exactly what this difference is we are not told. But Daniel 11 may provide a clue.

In Daniel 11 and the story of the vile person as was previously mentioned it becomes increasingly obvious as the chapter unfolds that this is a reference to the Antichrist after he resurrects from the dead. However, there is a statement within that verse that may inform us why the Antichrist is considered different. We are told "they will not give the <u>honor of royalty</u>" to the vile person… the Antichrist. He not receiving the honor of royalty, and this fact being significant enough to be noted in scripture, indicates some kind of an issue relating to him relative to royal lineage. So his being different from the ten may be related to princely royalty of which he is not, but perhaps the ten princes are. This is speculation as the Hebrew word for royalty is "malkut" which can also mean kingdom instead of royalty. Then there is the power play.

It is clear that as the Antichrist strives for the throne of this different beast kingdom he will not have the support of all ten princes initially. He has to subdue three of them. But it is equally apparent that after doing so those three return to his good graces. This is because we are told all ten are destined to possess literal kingdoms made up of the conquered lands. Revelation 17 also tells us all ten are of one mind, and they will give their power and authority to the beast. And all ten are also destined to receive authority for one hour as kings with the beast. This power play wherein the Antichrist overcomes and then restores three kings appears to be a reflection of some kind of internal political intrigue within the beast kingdom. And it is ripe for speculation. Relating to the three he overcomes the Hebrew verb "shephal" is used for subdue and it essentially means to humble. Whereas a few verses earlier we are told of those three they "were plucked out by the roots." Indicating a much rougher handling of them will initially take place before they come to their dark senses in support of the Antichrist.

The restoration of the three princes or leaders whom he will pluck out or humble may be related to his needing to placate some of the ten due to being different from them. We know part of his difference is that the ten have longevity greater than his within the beast kingdom since we are told Antichrist shall rise after them. Or it could be that all ten have such strong power bases within the beast kingdom that he has no choice. Remember, the beast kingdom is different from any other kingdom in history. Fundamentally different. The restoration of those three whom the Antichrist subdues is likely born of some kind of practical political necessity. Such political necessities may also explain why all ten are granted the title of king at the time they exalt him to the throne. Consider again the strange nature of that verse: "but they receive authority for one hour as kings with the beast."

Even though their authority is whisked away only an hour after it is granted, what likely remains is the title of king. The exalted title may be part of a compromise — a political payoff of sorts — as part of the effort to satisfy factions among these princes to pull together the support of all ten. Granting them the title of king is an incredible honor. This is done before they become actual kings with a geographical kingdom in the fulfillment of the yet part of Revelation 17. Although these ten will surely covet the title of king, the Antichrist likely has another reason for this title being granted. As previously mentioned he likely wants to be able to say he is the king of kings. Whether or not the ten are aware that the future holds actual kingdoms for them we cannot know. But it is likely that as the Antichrist works his way to the throne of the beast kingdom he has already developed his plan to conquer the world. So what better carrot to dangle before the ten than the promise of actual kingdoms in the future. Not just the title of king accompanied by an hour of actual power. But there is more.

Since these ten princes or leaders are in strong political positions within the beast kingdom before the Antichrist's rise, he would need to possess an impressive set of persuasion skills to outwit and overcome them. Power politics demands this. Such skills would appear to relate to the beastly nature of the Antichrist as described by the prophets. Daniel chapter 8 describes him as having "fierce features." Exactly what those features are we are not told. However, we do know that from the perspective of men he is viewed as fierce. Typically such fierceness instills fear. Daniel 7 sums up the impact of his appearance by simply saying it is "greater than his fellows." And this physical appearance is combined with an uncanny understanding of sinister schemes making his ability to outmaneuver opponents unmatched. Scripture describes him as having an understanding of dark sentences meaning he not only has an uncanny ability to understand the most difficult riddles and perplexing questions but also dark and obscure utterances leaving the ten princes/kings hopelessly outgunned as well as completely impressed. This probably explains why only three oppose the usurper rising within this strangely different beast kingdom to ultimately rule it. As for the seven who do not oppose him, they are so impressed that they set aside their political ambitions in support of him and ultimately receive a large demonic payoff. Becoming actual "kings" over parts of the conquered lands. And those lands will be massive. But such demonic understandings and fierceness can come from only one source. Satan.

His power shall be mighty, but not by his own power.
Daniel 8:24

Daniel goes on to describe how destructive he will be. But despite his destructiveness, or perhaps because of it, he "shall prosper and thrive." And in line with understanding difficult riddles and dark sentences, he is cunning and "shall cause deceit to prosper under his rule." Through dark understandings derived supernaturally from Satan, he is the most treacherous leader to ever walk the earth. That says a lot considering the litany of monsters history has unleashed on unsuspecting generations. This is what these ten princes are up against and they are no match. But what is this beast kingdom that Antichrist takes over? The one that is unlike any that has ever before existed on the earth.

CHAPTER SIX

The Beast Kingdom

Some of what was considered in the previous chapter will
repeated here in reaching additional conclusions.

In the previous chapter, we saw several characteristics of the beast kingdom as described by the prophets. Perhaps the most notable detail
is given by the prophet Daniel when he tells us it will be unlike any
kingdom that has existed in history. As such followers of Christ must
think in terms that are completely different when seeking to identify it.
In continuing to explore this difference it is helpful to first consider what
it is not. The difference cannot be related to its strange characteristics
described in the Books of Daniel and Revelation. Those colorful descriptions of seven heads, ten horns and the likeness of a lion, leopard and bear
when deciphered, are not unusual to kingdoms at all. That is because the
seven heads are simply a succession of kings leading to the Antichrist.
With himself being both the sixth and the eighth king. Although his return from the dead is highly unusual — accounting for his attaining the
throne twice — kings succeeding one another are not. Nor is it unusual
for a kingdom to have allies. Such allies as the lion, leopard and bear are
common to all empires. As for the ten horns who are ten kings minding
the lands conquered by the beast and under his thumb, this is no different

than the power structures used by Hitler, Caesar, Alexander and a host of leaders across time. Yet, we are told by Daniel that the beast kingdom…

… shall be different from all other kingdoms. Daniel 7:23

"Different." Yet, the colorful descriptions of it provided by the prophets present a kingdom much like that of past kingdoms. So this difference cannot relate to the succession of leadership, possession of allies or appointed rulers. The difference would appear to be on a more fundamental level. A type of kingdom that has never before existed. Now enters Satan the picture to sew confusion.

As we know Satan is the master of deception. His doomed legions relentlessly seek to lead people away from the Lord's truth. Unfortunately, those efforts to sew confusion into the church have succeeded on multiple fronts. And Bible prophecy has not been immune to it. Because Bible prophecy has so many moving parts and is so often spoken of in mysterious terms it is especially vulnerable to his attacks. A case in point relates to the rise of the Antichrist. What is widely taught today is the notion that he will arise out of a ten-nation confederacy. Such groupings of nations into alliances have existed in the past. This perspective has caused many to keep a watchful eye on the formation of nation groups with special attention directed toward the European Union. This teaching of Antichrist rising out of a ten nation confederacy primarily stems from the ten horns who are ten kings and the verse that says…

> The ten horns are ten kings
> <u>Who shall arise from this kingdom.</u>
> <u>And another shall rise after them;</u>
> He shall be different from the first ones,
> And shall subdue three kings. Daniel 7:24

It is accepted by many that since the Antichrist "shall rise after" these ten kings he, therefore, arises from within a group of ten nations led by these ten kings. That is the dominant teaching today. And a surface read of this scripture taken in isolation seems to support that conclusion. As a result, many of those embracing that teaching are feverishly looking for a ten-nation confederacy out of which the Antichrist will arise. But remember that Revelation 17 assures us the ten kings do not yet have kingdoms at the time they lift the Antichrist to the throne of the beast kingdom. In line with that in a closer look at Daniel 7, we see that these ten kings arise from within a single kingdom... "Who shall arise from this kingdom." Singular. Perfectly consistent with the statement of Revelation 17. And that detail seems to be overlooked by many. In other words, the rise of the ten kings' to possess actual kingdoms takes place from within the beast kingdom itself — when it is still a singular entity. The wording of the scripture says they arise from "this kingdom" and not "these kingdoms." Truth is most often found in detail. These clear scriptural statements of truth throw a monkey wrench into the notion that the ten kings each possess ten separate kingdoms as the Antichrist rises to the beast throne.

Revelation 17:12 makes it clear that... "The ten horns which you saw are ten kings who have received no kingdom as yet." They don't yet have a kingdom at the time they exalt Antichrist to the throne of the beast kingdom. Yet indicates they each will eventually have an actual kingdom to rule. But not at the time they raise Antichrist to the throne. So when Daniel 7:24 states that these "ten kings ... shall arise from this kingdom," and Antichrist "shall rise after them," the events of Daniel 7:24 must take place before these ten kings have actual kingdoms based on Revelation 17:12. But these ten kings or princes/leaders are clearly significant players within the strange and different beast kingdom before the rise of Antichrist. And the beast kingdom is a singular entity at that point in time.

This is the first glimpse of how the beast kingdom is fundamentally different. In its beginning phase, before it starts conquering, its reach is so widespread that it already has ten significant leaders who will ultimately spawn into ten kings with actual kingdoms to rule. It is the most strange and different kind of kingdom in all of human history. It is fundamentally different. And this is the key point. The beast kingdom initially is not characterized by a ten-nation confederacy. The ten kings eventually become real kings out of this single kingdom — the beast kingdom — but only after Antichrist rises above them within it. And that is worth repeating. All ten as well as the Antichrist arise from this single kingdom. Not a ten-nation confederacy as many teach. The ten kingdom confederacy comes later. After the Antichrist rises to power.

The ten obviously possess significant status within the beast kingdom at the time Antichrist becomes a noteworthy figure there. Since we are told he rises after them it would appear he is some kind of usurper relative to their status within the kingdom. And this has to cause friction within the ranks of the ten. In fact, Daniel states "He shall be different" from the ten. Whatever the difference it likely adds to the friction between Antichrist and the ten.

As noted in the previous chapter the lands/nations/regions these ten kings will ultimately rule will almost certainly come as a result of the success Antichrist scores when he rides the white horse of Revelation 6 conquering and to conquer. He is able to ride the white horse because the ten placed him upon it by enthroning him at the time they held lesser positions within the beast kingdom. Before they have kingdoms of their own. Then he transforms those ten princes/leaders into actual kings after his conquering. That creates the ten-kingdom confederacy taught within prophecy circles. It is important to remember scripture simply refers to the ten by the ultimate office they eventually hold… kings. And not by the lesser office they held along the way… princes as covered in the last chapter based on Isaiah 10. This is in the same manner as we do today. It also points to another Antichrist delusion wherein he tries to mimic Jesus as a kind of king of kings by making the ten all kings when they lift him up to the throne.

All of this leads to the conclusion that what the Antichrist actually arises from is this mysterious beast kingdom. At the point in time wherein he rises to the throne there is no ten-kingdom confederacy… yet. It is a kingdom that is different from all other kingdoms. At least part of this dif-ference must be that it is massively widespread even before the Antichrist taking the throne and conquering. This is indicated by it already having ten very significant leaders within it. Yet, it is a single kingdom or entity of some kind. "Different" as Daniel would say. These ten princes or major leaders obviously have significant positions of power within this different kingdom before the Antichrist rises within it. And that is revealing. It raises the question of how big the beast kingdom must be in order to house ten very significant leaders even before Antichrist rises to the throne and begins conquering. This would appear to indicate that it must be very widespread across the earth.

The concept that there is a ten-nation confederacy from which the Antichrist rises instead of a single beast kingdom is a significant decep-tion sewn by Satan. One that is destined to cause his identity to remain shrouded in mystery much longer than it needs to be. As such after he arises many in the church will claim he cannot be the Antichrist since he did not come out of a ten-nation confederacy. This will be the case despite the massive power he will wield against mankind as he persecutes Christians. Such power Daniel noted as he wrote about the fourth beast — the beast kingdom.

> ...shall devour the whole earth,
> Trample it and break it in pieces. Daniel 7:23

The power of the beast kingdom is over the "whole earth." With such power as to take the world and "trample it and break it in pieces." This too indicates a widespread power base that is fundamentally different from any single kingdom that has ever before existed. And the number of ac-complices required to achieve such an undertaking should be breathtaking indicating a worldwide infrastructure of elite leaders dedicated to bending the knee to his wicked will. Since we are told he will rule the whole earth, then the ten kings he appoints to oversee it would likely already have status and/or name recognition in each of the kingdom regions they are granted kingship over. From a practical political perspective, this would be necessary to help pacify the conquered masses by having a familiar name and face over them. Additionally, the deceptive nature of mass media would almost certainly come into play to convince the subjugated masses that they are experiencing some form of true democracy. This narrative would gather support from a segment of citizens who are more able to be manipulated. Such citizens and elites would march in dark lockstep and singlemindedness of purpose toward a delusional common goal. And this is where Daniel 7 appears to come back into play. At the time wherein the ten kings exalt Antichrist to his throne, we are told…

…These are of one mind… Daniel 7:13

And this one mindedness will likely be the norm for elites and citizens across the world who form the wretched backbone of the beast kingdom. All of this leads to the conclusion that the fundamental difference Daniel speaks of may be that the beast kingdom is not a nation-state. But a kingdom without borders that consists of massive political, media, corporate, and cultural power elites colluding toward a common goal. Such a kingdom would not only be more powerful than any other in history, having a worldwide power base with powerful regional leaders but possess the fundamental difference Daniel spoke of. A kingdom without borders that over time grows in strength and wicked singlemindedness until it finally metastasizes to conquer the world as its leader rides the white horse of Revelation 6 conquering and to conquer. Such a kingdom would be able to exert influence in every nation fulfilling Daniel 7:7

It was granted to him to make war with the saints and to overcome them. And authority was given him over every tribe, tongue, and nation.

For centuries rumors have abounded that such an entity exists and that its power was growing. There has even evolved a generally accepted name for this world power order. It is referred to by many as the New World

Order. A powerful supranational entity made up of world elites who elevate their minions into the leadership positions of nations, media, corporations and major institutions across the globe. And there is today anecdotal evidence that something wicked like it does exists. Such evidence comes in many forms. One such piece of evidence is the grip of authoritarian control over mass media which now promotes a single-minded narrative that so often conflicts with observable reality. It also promotes morals and beliefs that are anti-God and it appears to be rife with Satanism.

There is also an observable effort on the part of governments to gain maximum control over the lives of those they rule. Although this is to be expected from certain countries, the difference now is the coordinated effort on a worldwide basis indicating some kind of devilish common thread connecting world leaders, corporations, media and major institutions. And this coordinated effort is not limited to the lives of individuals. But also directed toward nation-states as well. Any small country that does not bend the knee to the will of this international group will typically face a propaganda onslaught followed by armed invasion. Thereafter, a puppet regime is placed in power. Typically all of this is done in the name of democracy. If the nation rebelling cannot easily be invaded then crushing economic sanctions are leveled.

Whatever this entity is it is very real, dark and different from anything mankind has ever before faced. An entity without conscience, but with a clear drive toward total control. A new kind of godless kingdom that is wicked to its core. A massively powerful kingdom with many leaders, but no set borders. Until, of course, the Antichrist rides the white horse of Revelation 6 going about conquering and to conquer establishing regional kingdoms led by his princes making them kings.

But all of this raises another obvious question. How can the Antichrist pull off conquering a world filled with militarily powerful nations such as the United States? And this is where his understanding of dark sentences and devious plots come into play.

CHAPTER SEVEN

Trojan Horses

According to various scriptures, the Antichrist is an "Assyrian" and he is wickedly crafty. Described by the Lord as "the rod of My anger" in Isaiah 10, the Antichrist will be used by God as "the staff of His indignation." Joel 3:2 tells us this indignation is expressed in the Valley of Jehoshaphat — the theatre of the Lord's judgment where all nations are gathered for the great war launching the birth pangs beginning of the day of the Lord — the end times. Revelation 6 tells of the Antichrist riding the white horse in the beginning as he goes about conquering and to conquer. But it is in Isaiah 13 where we are told how the wicked man overcomes the nations of the world from this strange and different beast kingdom that he rules. And in so doing he acquires the lands necessary to appoint his ten princes to be rulers of actual kingdoms in fulfillment of the prophecies telling us that they will ultimately be kings with kingdoms.

It is a tactic made famous in mythology. It was Odysseus and his Greeks who hid inside a wooden horse brought within the walls of gloating Troy, too busy celebrating the gift to be aware of the treachery that lay within. Falling prey to their pride. Once inside the impregnable walls protecting the city the small band of Greeks opened the gate ensuring its destruction. Like the Greeks of mythology so too will the Antichrist strike nations from within using his own Trojan horses. People from

another land are allowed within the walls of the nations they are destined
to destroy.

> 5 They come from a far country, from the end of heaven,
> even the LORD, and the weapons of his indignation, to
> destroy the whole land. Isaiah 13:5

The land they come from is a "far country" from the lands they live
in and ultimately destroy. Although we are colorfully told they come
"from the end of heaven," this is a term similar to that also used in Ne.
1:8-9, Dan. 8:8-9, and Jer. 49:36 and each time it means across the earth
and not the Lord's abode of heaven. They are the Lord's "weapons of His
indignation" of His wrath. And within what time frame of the end times
does this take place?

> 8 And they will be afraid.
> Pangs and sorrows will take hold of them;
> They will be in pain as a woman in childbirth...
> Isaiah 13:8

Birth pangs. We are simply being told who it is during the birth pangs
beginning of the end times that strike the nations of the earth bringing
them to their weakened knees. It is those living within the attacked nations who come from a far country. This is because the Antichrist cannot
overcome powerful nations by directly confronting them. There are too
many and they are too well armed. But even mighty men full of strength
can be brought to their knees by craft. And Antichrist is the master of
craft and dark sentences. He uses deceit and cunning to take down those
thought to be impregnable. "They come from a far country... to destroy
the whole land." And their attack will cause the great war to launch birth
pangs bringing all nations to the full end Jeremiah talks about. They are
his suicidal warriors awaiting the order to attack. But after unleashing
torrents of fire and hell on the nations that took them in these hunters

become the hunted. They suddenly become like "the hunted gazelle" that must "flee to his own land. Everyone" of them!

> [14] It shall be as the hunted gazelle, And as a sheep that no man takes up; Every man will turn to his own people, And everyone will flee to his own land. Isaiah 13:14

They flee for good reason. The people of their host countries will understand who was behind the attack and target them as a group causing their mass exodus. Such that everyone will flee to his own land. And this raises the specter that the attack they launch will be of the highest order in severity as nothing less would cause such a radical response from the citizens of the attacked nations. The innocent will be targeted with the guilty. So great will be the rage of those attacked that...

> [15] Everyone who is found will be thrust through, And everyone who is captured will fall by the sword. [16] Their children also will be dashed to pieces before their eyes; Their houses will be plundered And their wives ravished. Isaiah 13:15-16

A murderous rampage of rage unleashes against those from a far country suspected of being behind the attacks. So severe is this response that even... "Their children also will be dashed to pieces before their eyes." Their property will be plundered along with their wives. But there is something odd here. Public rage is not tolerated by governments to manifest into such widespread mayhem. And that raises the specter of anarchy. Apparently the attacks are so severe that governments are unable to restore order. As such since there is no protection, "every man will turn to his own people, And everyone will flee to his own land." The people from a far country, who include the attackers, flee back to their countries of origin. The flow of events is clear. But how can such Trojan horses ignite a level of destruction necessary to fulfill these passages as well as conquer a multitude of nations for the rider of the white horse? The answer appears in 2 Peter 3:10.

> ¹⁰ But the day of the Lord will <u>come as a thief in the night</u>; in the which the heavens shall pass away with a great noise, and the elements shall melt with fervent heat, the earth also and the works that are therein shall be burned up. 2 Peter 3:10

The sudden destruction of the day of the Lord described in 1 Thessalonians 5:1-3 comes as a thief in the night. And as we know this marks the beginning of the end times. Birth pangs. 2 Peter 3:10 uses that same thief in the night phrase also in describing the day of the Lord. What is described is nothing less than nuclear devastation. This makes sense. It is the detonation of nuclear weapons smuggled within their host nations by warriors of the Antichrist. And they devastate the most powerful nations on earth from within. Against such attacks, there is no defense. As the master of dark sentences, such an attack is perfectly in line with his wicked nature. (The Epilogue at the back of the book relays a dream from the Lord given to this author relating to a specific detail of this beginning attack.)

This is the same beginning Revelation 6 describes as the four horsemen of the apocalypse galloping on their devastating ride. It is the full end Jeremiah 30 tells us is dealt against all nations. Joel informs us all nations are taken into the Valley of Jehoshaphat — the theatre of God's judgment. Jesus tells us nation shall rise against nation and kingdom against kingdom in Matthew 24:7. This is all just the beginning... birth pangs.

Because we are told it is foreigners living within countries who are used by God against all nations, it is clear that the most vulnerable countries to this tactic are the Western democracies. Nations whose borders have been almost non-existent for decades. And this conclusion dove-tails with Zephaniah describing those hardest hit.

Western Nations

War is fickle hitting some harder than others. And according to the prophet Zephaniah (1:14), this great war will be no different. Instead of using a birth pangs term to identify the beginning of the day of the Lord, he simply states "the great day of the Lord is near; It is near and hastens quickly." Tellingly he describes "the noise of the day of the Lord is bitter" — the descriptive used by Peter 3:10 inferring one of the main characteristics of nuclear detonations. He then describes certain nations that are hit especially hard when the great war launches. Their notable characteristic is that they possess the best national defenses, intelligence services and are wealthy.

> [16]A day of the trumpet and alarm against the <u>fenced cities</u>, and against the <u>high towers</u>. Zephaniah 1:16

"Fenced cities" signify notable military protection. "High towers" indicate notable intelligence services. And these are wealthy nations. Because "neither their silver nor their gold shall be able to deliver them in the day of the Lord's wrath; but the whole land shall be devoured." (1:18) These nations are consumed by fire and it comes from those of a far country attacking from within. The result is that the nations face Jeremiah's full end from these attacks. And those descriptions best fit America and Western Europe. It is this Western block of nations that possesses the strongest military and intelligence services as well as the greatest wealth.

The New Ruler

When the devastating birth pangs are over it is the Antichrist who is on top. As for all nations, it is a very different story. They have just been trampled by the four horsemen of the apocalypse. Vanquished by a crafty foe who excels in dark sentences and devious plans. With the birth pangs beginning phase of the day of the Lord complete other players enter the prophetic picture. And this picture requires some speculation centered on timing.

Perhaps now some of the devastated nations have become vassal states of the newly expanded beast kingdom. With the threat of more nuclear devastation hanging like a sword over the heads of national leaders, not knowing which of their major cities could experience nuclear detonations next, the conquered must bend the knee to the new ruler. And because of the number of nations conquered it is likely that regional kingdoms spring up out of the chaos of birth pangs. We know from Revelation 13 that ultimately "all the world ... followed the beast." Perhaps at this early stage, his princes are already becoming kings over the conquered lands. What we do know is that they will ultimately become ten kings with literal kingdoms to rule. Precisely when this happens is uncertain. As for the three nations destined to become Antichrist's major allies: the loathsome lion, leopard and bear, perhaps seeing his victories over a multitude of nations they begin moving toward him in dark alliance at this point. We know from Daniel 7 that this will eventually take place. But one thing is certain. After birth pangs the world power structure is flipped on its head.

The Peace Agreement Problem

As for the Antichrist, there is yet another action he must undertake after birth pangs are over and it relates to the Peace agreement initiated by all nations. The one that removed land from the Jews triggering the birth pangs beginning of the day of the Lord. Removing the land deeded to them by God. The agreement has a problem. We understand this from the fact that for some reason the Antichrist must confirm or strengthen it for seven years according to Daniel 9:27. Exactly what the problem is we are not told. But the fact that he involves himself in a reappraisal of the agreement — extending it for seven years — indicates something is up with it that must be dealt with. And it is noteworthy that although it was all nations who initiated the agreement before birth pangs. After birth pangs it is the Antichrist who replaces them as the authority over it. And this makes perfect sense. All nations are left devastated after birth pangs. But there is good reason the Antichrist becomes involved in rehashing the agreement. It is part of his sinister plan. A plan to maneuver the Jews into rebuilding the "temple of God."

Temple Construction

We see in Revelation 11 the first reference to the rebuilt Jewish temple as well as an instrument of construction — "a measuring rod" — and a reference to the first half of the seven years — "forty-two months."

> Then I was given a reed like <u>a measuring rod</u>. And the angel stood, saying, "<u>Rise</u> and measure the <u>temple of God</u>, the altar, and those who worship there. [2] But leave out the court which is outside the temple, and do not measure it, for it has been given to the Gentiles. And they will tread the holy city underfoot for <u>forty-two months</u>. Revelation 11:1-2

In Strong's Concordance the Greek word for "rise" is the verb "egeiro" which when used in reference to a building means: "to raise up, construct, erect." In conjunction with a tool of construction — a measuring rod — Revelation 11:1-2 would appear to indicate the rebuilding of the temple takes place during the first half of the seven years — forty-two months — and not before. If correct then that means construction does not start until after the Antichrist confirms or strengthens the initial Peace agreement by all nations for those seven years. And that is interesting. When considering the plan of the Antichrist to sit in the rebuilt temple of God pretending to be a god — according to 2 Thessalonians 2 — it is likely he is the one who initiates a reappraisal of the original agreement. In fact, in order to grant a seven-year extension of that agreement he may insist upon the Jews rebuilding the temple. Since we know in advance his plan to sit in the rebuilt temple and defile it, and it appears to be rebuilt during the first half of the seven years — only after "he shall confirm the covenant with many for one week" — the likelihood that the rebuilding of the temple of God is part of confirming the original agreement for those seven years would appear quite high. And, of course, having longed for their temple for two thousand years the Jews will be more than happy to comply.

All of this also indicates why he is not be aggressive against Israel during the first half of the seven years. The Antichrist needs Israel to rebuild their temple without fear or threat so it is fully consecrated to the Lord before he defiles it. That is why it is only after the mid-point of the seven years — after he desecrates the temple — wherein Revelation 12 tells us he is in hot pursuit of Israel.

CHAPTER EIGHT

The Seven Years: The First Half

When the four horsemen of the apocalypse begin their ferocious ride unleashing torrents of wars, famines, diseases, earthquakes, and celestial horrors, the birth pangs beginning of the day of the Lord has arrived. But their ride is only the beginning of what mankind faces. Birth pangs are only a forerunner to a birth. And prophetic birth pangs are no different. From the womb of Bible prophecy, these birth pangs produce the seven-year tribulation. Along with it the foul and odious reign of the Antichrist. His malevolent rule beginning sometime before "he shall confirm the covenant with many for one week," and then finally reaching its fiery end at the Battle of Armageddon completing that last week of years. It is the culmination of God's plan spoken of by the prophet Daniel.

Daniel's prophecy is the most significant and broadly encompassing one in the Bible. Called the "70 weeks" prophecy it compresses the Lord's plan for mankind into a period of 70 weeks of years or 490. But they are not contiguous weeks. They are separated in time with the final week of years representing the seven-year tribulation to be unleashed sometime in the future.

In addition to the unfolding horrors of those last seven years, there is the eventual redemption of Israel. The Jews finally accept the One they previously pierced. It is a miraculous coming around for the chosen people in fulfillment of God's plan. In fact, according to Revelation 7, the Lord finds within Israel 144,000 Jews, twelve thousand each from the twelve tribes, and they minister His truth about Jesus Christ to their fellow countrymen.

But before they begin their ministry an "angel ascending from the east, having the seal of the living God" finds each one of them and applies the Lord's protective seal "on their foreheads." This is the same seal all believers possess protecting each from the Lord's wrath touching them in this life or the next. This is necessary because what is about to unfold is nothing less than horrific. Yet, like the Israelites during the time of Pharaoh, as the Lord's wrath pours down all about them, it touches not a single hair on their heads. They are sealed!

According to Revelation 14 these 144,000 "are the ones who were not defiled with women, for they are virgins." They are pure and because of this purity, they are usable by God. They will eventually "sing as it were a new song before the throne, before the four living creatures, and the elders; and no one could learn that song except the hundred and forty-four thousand who were redeemed from the earth." During their ministry a multitude of terrors found in the Book of Revelation unfold across the earth. When their ministry is completed they are destined to be "firstfruits to God and to the Lamb" eventually being "redeemed from the earth" according to Revelation 14.

The brutal Book of Revelation in all its horrors unfolds from the loosening of seven seals. It is by the hand of Jesus they are undone. And there is a clear distinction among these seals. The first six unfold within a single chapter — Revelation 6. That is the chapter that matches the birth pangs described by Jesus in Matthew 24:7. The last seal — the seventh — is not released until two chapters later in chapter 8. And this separation of the seventh seal from the first six is not by accident. It is to stress the separate nature of birth pangs from the seven-year tribulation. Birth pangs birth the seven-year tribulation and, as a result, must be separate from it and before it.

Although the seventh seal is only one seal out of seven that observation does it no justice. It carries more punch than all six seals before it. That is because from it flow the seven trumpet judgments as well as the seven bowl judgments. And as bad as prophetic birth pangs are the actual baby born from them is incomparably worse in both longevity and severity. Welcome to the seven-year tribulation.

Silence in Heaven

Silence in heaven must be unusual. Because upon the opening of the seventh seal, we are told "there was silence in heaven for about half an hour." Interestingly, the combination of the first six seals which unleash the four horsemen did not have a similar effect. Only the seventh.

> When He opened the seventh seal, there was silence in heaven for about half an hour. Revelation 8:1

Such silence would appear to indicate something profound has happened. Something far more significant than even the horsemen of the Apocalypse could produce. This is because the seven-year tribulation springs forth from the seventh seal. It signals the final scene of a cosmic battle viewed from the bleachers of heaven since the serpent invaded Eden. And as the forces of heaven look on there appear "seven angels who stand before God, and to them were given seven trumpets." Now the scene in heaven turns surreal.

Another angel appears. He is holding a "golden censer." It contains "the prayers of the saints." He filled it "with fire from the altar, and threw it to the earth." And this produces "noises, thunderings, lightnings, and an earthquake." His mission is to prepare the way for the seven angels to sound their ruthless trumpets that will leave the earth in shambles. As one after another of those seven sound their trumpets, the earth will be afflicted with one plague after another unfolding over the first half of the seven-year tribulation.

The first angel sounds. And upon the earth rains down something not seen since the day Moses challenged Pharaoh. "Hail and fire... mingled with blood." It was "fire mingled with hail" that was the plague of old. Now the Lord has added blood to this arrow in His quiver. The impact is horrific. "A third of the trees are burned up, and all green grass." Immediately scripture describes the impact of the sounding of the second trumpet.

It appears in space and looks "like a great mountain burning with fire." It is heading straight for the earth. And as though projected by the hand of God it is "thrown into the sea." The result is cataclysmic. The shock waves across the surface of the oceans take down "a third of the ships." They are destroyed. The shock waves under the surface cause "a third of the living creatures in the sea" to die. And when the wretched rock from space is finished it leaves "a third of the sea blood." A grotesque memorial to the second angel.

The cosmos continues to issue forth His wrath. When the third angel sounds "a great star fell from heaven, burning like a torch." It brings with it a bitterness that infects "a third of the rivers and on the springs of water." As a result "many men died from the water, because it was made bitter." The star has a name. It is called Wormwood.

As if to emphasize the smallness of man and the Lord's rule over the planet he inhabits, the sounding of the fourth angel causes the lights in the sky to be darkened. Of the sun, moon, and stars "a third of them were darkened." But not just in the evening sky. "A third of the day did not shine, and likewise the night."

As all this destruction unfolds across a ravaged and shuttering earth, like an announcer at a great event an angel "flying through the midst of heaven" declares to its occupants with a loud voice "Woe, woe, woe to the inhabitants of the earth, because of the remaining blasts of the trumpet of the three angels who are about to sound!" He is preparing onlookers in heaven not just for the severity of the remaining trumpet judgments, but also their uniquely strange and twisted nature. They are as odd as they are severe issuing forth from the imagination of a God whose long suffering of man has finally come to an end. The fifth angel sounds.

There is a bottomless pit containing unspeakable entities. Within its horrid confines, these fearsome creatures have waited since the early days of the angelic rebellion. They are dark and powerful angels who violated their place and in turn, were thrown into this pit with each given a cloak of chains to wear. Now their time has arrived. "A star falls from heaven to the earth. To him was given the key to the bottomless pit." Upon opening its ancient gate "smoke arose out of the pit like the smoke of a great furnace. So the sun and the air were darkened because of the smoke of the pit"...

> ³ Then out of the smoke locusts came upon the earth. And to them was given power, as the scorpions of the earth have power. ⁴ They were commanded not to harm the grass of the earth, or any green thing, or any tree, but only those men who do not have the seal of God on their foreheads. ⁵ And they were not given authority to kill them, but to torment them for five months. Their torment was like the torment of a scorpion when it strikes a man. ⁶ In those days men will seek death and will not find it; they will desire to die, and death will flee from them.
> Revelation 9:3-6

The destruction of the green grass that took place during the first trumpet has passed. There has been regrowth. Although the new grass and trees are spared by this trumpet mankind is not. Those whose foreheads are sealed by God get a pass. And that includes the one hundred and forty-four thousand. Although God's wrath rains down his children are not touched by it. But as for those who are not sealed, there is no escape from the swarming locusts that are released by the trumpeter. Those tormented "will seek death and will not find it; they will desire to die, and death will flee from them." It is not just what the locusts do that is a menace.

Their appearance terrifies. They are the complete package designed by the all-knowing God of heaven whose imagination is infinite.

> 7 The shape of the locusts was like horses prepared for battle. On their heads were crowns of something like gold, and their faces were like the faces of men. 8 They had hair like women's hair, and their teeth were like lions' teeth. 9 And they had breastplates like breastplates of iron, and the sound of their wings was like the sound of chariots with many horses running into battle. Revelation 9:7-9

Perhaps this is a nanotech nightmare. Or simply Divine imagination becomes reality. But to those affected, it matters not. Their torment is the same. And these waves of flying curses have a king over them. It is the angel of the bottomless pit, "whose name in Hebrew is Abaddon, but in Greek he has the name Apollyon." Might this Apollyon released from the bottomless pit be the same fallen angel whom we are told in Revelation 17 comes up from the bottomless pit to possess the Antichrist when he resurrects after suffering the fatal wound? We can only wonder as the pit is home to a great company of fallen angels.

When the sixth angel sounds the picture that initially appears is difficult for the mind of man to process. At "the golden alter which is before God... four horns" speak with one voice. They are speaking to the angel with the sixth trumpet. They command doom to be issued from the release of four angels who have been "bound at the great river Euphrates." Those angels have been waiting "for the hour and day and month and year... to kill a third of mankind." Their wait is over. From those four angels rises an army the like of which mankind has never before seen. It is fearsome in both appearance and number. There are two hundred million of them. All are horsemen. And they are very strange horsemen.

For all his brutality the Mongolian leader Genghis Kahn never had horsemen like these. Their heads are "like the heads of lions; and out of their mouths came fire, smoke, and brimstone." And they are powerful. "Their power is in their mouth and in their tails; for their tails are like serpents, having heads; and with them they do harm." Those riding them dress in the colors of war. "Breastplates of fiery red, hyacinth blue, and sulfur yellow." Yet, despite of their horrific unleashing of death, the hardened hearts of mankind do...

> ...not repent of the works of their hands, that they should not worship demons, and idols of gold, silver, brass, stone, and wood, which can neither see nor hear nor walk. [21] And they did not repent of their murders or their sorceries or their sexual immorality or their thefts. Revelation 9:20-21

The great surreal artist Pablo Picasso could not do justice to the picture Revelation 10 is about to paint. It leaves the mind of man grasping for a reference. The chapter does not cover the sounding of the seventh trumpet. It simply sets the stage for it.

I saw still another mighty angel coming down from heaven, clothed with a cloud. And a rainbow was on his head, his face was like the sun, and his feet like pillars of fire. [2] He had a little book open in his hand. And he set his right foot on the sea and his left foot on the land, [3] and cried with a loud voice, as when a lion roars. When he cried out, seven thunders uttered their voices. [4] Now when the seven thunders uttered their voices, I was about to write; but I heard a voice from heaven saying to me, "Seal up the things which the seven thunders uttered, and do not write them." Revelation 10:1-4

Powerful and strange angels are everywhere. This one's garment is a cloud. His shining face has a rainbow above and strange feet... of fire below. His voice causes seven thunders to begin revealing secrets no man is allowed to know. Then swearing by Him Who lives forever the angel declares...

> [7] but in the days of the sounding of the seventh angel,
> when he is about to sound, the mystery of God would
> be finished, as He declared to His servants the prophets.
> Revelation 10:7

The trumpet of the seventh angel is the last trumpet. And after it sounds we are told "the mystery of God would be finished." Mysteries abound. (This mysterious verse is unraveled in "The Resurrection of the Dead and The Rapture" chapter.)

The same voice that commands the words of the seven thunders to be sealed now issues a new command. John is to take a "little book which is open in the hand of the angel who stands on the sea and on the earth." He is then told to eat it. He does. After doing so the angel issues him a new command: "You must prophesy again about many peoples, nations, tongues, and kings."

Already mankind is deep into the first half of the seven-year tribulation and the seventh angel has not yet blown his trumpet. In the meantime, as the first six trumpets unleashed their punishing blows against a world already battered by the four horsemen, other significant prophetic events have been unfolding alongside them.

> Then I was given a reed like a measuring rod. And the
> angel stood, saying, "Rise and measure the temple of God,
> the altar, and those who worship there. [2] But leave out the
> court which is outside the temple, and do not measure
> it, for it has been given to the Gentiles. And they will tread
> the holy city underfoot for forty-two months.
> Revelation 11:1-2

This is the first reference to the rebuilt Jewish temple in the Book of Revelation. And it is a critical piece of the prophetic puzzle that must be in place before the Antichrist "sits as God in the temple of God, showing himself that he is God," according to 2 Thessalonians 2. This sitting in the temple by the dark one is a major offense to the Holy One and takes place at the midpoint of the seven years. We are also told what is happening to Jerusalem across the first half of the seven years. The "Gentiles… will tread the holy city underfoot for forty-two months." The word used for tread is the Greek verb "pateo." And the key to understanding the significance of this treading of the holy city is found in Luke 21:24:

> …And Jerusalem will be trampled by Gentiles until the
> times of the Gentiles are fulfilled.

Since Revelation 11 informs us that "Gentles… will tread the holy city underfoot for forty-two months" — the first half of the seven years — then based on Luke 21 we know the "times of the Gentiles" continue across that time frame. The word used for trampled in Luke is the same Greek verb "pateo" as used in Revelation 11. But there is something else that has been happening during the entire first half of those seven years. Two very strange figures have appeared on the world stage. They are the strangest persons ever to walk the earth. They are supernatural. Empowered by God. They are prophets. And their great powers are used to wreak more havoc.

> ³ And I will appoint my two witnesses, and they will
> prophesy for 1,260 days, clothed in sackcloth." ⁴ They are
> "the two olive trees" and the two lampstands, and "they
> stand before the Lord of the earth."

Whereas the Gentiles are trampling Jerusalem for "42 months" — the first half of the seven years — so too does the ministry of these two witnesses span that time frame — "1,260 days." The trigger for their appearance is the launch of the seven years — itself triggered when the Antichrist "confirms the covenant with many." And, of course, the "many" that originated the "Peace" agreement is "all nations." The United Nations.

Since the temple is also mentioned at the beginning of Revelation 11 — including a tool of construction — a "measuring rod" — and the Greek verb "egeiro" is used for "rise" which when used in reference to a building means "construct" — this appears to indicate the temple is rebuilt during the first half of the seven years. But as Revelation 11:2 tells us: "leave out the court which is outside the temple, and do not measure it, for it has been given to the Gentiles." Might the court which is outside the temple be where the Islamic Dome of the Rock now sits? A building on which its walls are inscriptions denying Christ. In any event, the temple must be completed by the mid-point for the Antichrist to sit in and defile. As for those two witnesses...

> ⁵ If anyone tries to harm them, fire comes from their mouths and devours their enemies. This is how anyone who wants to harm them must die. ⁶ They have power to shut up the heavens so that it will not rain during the time they are prophesying; and they have power to turn the waters into blood and to strike the earth with every kind of plague as often as they want. Revelation 11:3-6

Flames of death are the wages issued to those attacking them — a fate of cinder and ash for the enemies of God. These witnesses are an extension of God's wrath causing rain to cease, "to turn the waters into blood," and they can issue any plague they desire. And they have great desire. As the world suffers in their grip nothing can stop their testimony of prophecy from being completed. Nothing. But when they are finished the beast from "the Abyss will attack them." This is the same bottomless pit from which Apollyon rises through its smoke. God lets this "beast from the Abyss overpower and kill the two witnesses." But He is setting a trap.

> ⁷ Now when they have finished their testimony, the beast that comes up from the Abyss will attack them, and overpower and kill them. ⁸ Their bodies will lie in the public square of the great city—which is figuratively called Sodom and Egypt—where also their Lord was crucified. Revelation 11:7-8

The madness of the devil from the bottomless pit commands that their dead bodies "lie in the public square." Unburied. His minions crazed with the blood lust of demonic influence rejoice in delirium gurgled up from the bowels of hell.

> [9] For three and a half days some from every people, tribe, language and nation will gaze on their bodies and refuse them burial. [10] The inhabitants of the earth will gloat over them and will celebrate by sending each other gifts, because these two prophets had tormented those who live on the earth. Revelation 11

The beast from the Abyss and his followers think they have won this battle. They gloat over the "death" of the two witnesses and "celebrate by sending each other gifts." Their tormentors are dead! But their ravaged minds do not know the scriptures. Their joy is to be short-lived.

> [11] But after the three and a half days the breath of life from God entered them, and they stood on their feet, and terror struck those who saw them. [12] Then they heard a loud voice from heaven saying to them, "Come up here." And they went up to heaven in a cloud, while their enemies looked on. Revelation 11

In a stunning supernatural rebuke to the forces of darkness, the Lord resurrects His two witnesses. They stand on their feet. Terror strikes the hearts of their enemies. And the eyes of those enemies twisted in demonic rage and transfixed on their resurrected bodies hear "a loud voice from heaven" — "Come up here." And the witnesses disappear into the clouds. Their ministry is complete. Then in a Divine exclamation point "a severe earthquake" strikes Jerusalem killing "seven thousand." The seventh trumpet sounds.

Upon its sounding "loud voices in heaven" issue forth profound words. Joined by "twenty-four elders" who sit "before God on their thrones" and the God of heaven is praised. The scene becomes dramatic. "The temple of God is opened." Within it can be seen the "ark of the covenant" — the agreement God made with mankind. The opening of the temple is greeted with "flashes of lightning, rumblings, peals of thunder, an earthquake and a severe hailstorm." The first half of the seven-year tribulation is finished. Now an even greater cataclysm of judgments awaits unrepentant mankind.

CHAPTER NINE

The Seven Years: The Second Half

Just as the dawn flushes a new morning sky so too shall it be when the bell tolls to the mid-point of the seven years. At that moment a great blasphemy will usher in a new and even crueler era of days than those just past. After the sixth king (Antichrist) suffers the "deadly wound," and then amazes the world with his miraculous resurrection from the dead, Revelation 17:8 tells us "the beast that you saw was, and is not, and will ascend out of the bottomless pit." The cruel man will be possessed by the beast from the "bottomless pit" when he resurrects. If there was ever the slightest chance of reasoning with him that element has been consumed by the blackness of the pit resurrected within him. As such he begins a reign of demonic terror that dwarfs even that of the first half of the seven years.

The Lord's temple is special to Him. So much so that He would not allow faithful David to begin construction due to the amount of blood on his hands in dealing with enemies. That honor fell to his wise son Solomon. And once again during the end times, the Jewish temple will stand ready. Unwittingly rebuilt for a great desecration in fulfillment of Christian prophecy. The holy seat will be defiled by the shadow of the Antichrist who will sit "as God in the temple of God, showing himself that he is God" according to 2 Thessalonians 2:4. In His Olivet Discourse Jesus joins the prophet Daniel in referring to that desecration as the 'abomination of desolation.' Both Daniel 9:27 and Jesus in His Discourse identify the vindictive act as happening at the mid-point. And the result is devastating.

> [21] For then there will be great tribulation, such as has not been since the beginning of the world until this time, no, nor ever shall be. [22] And unless those days were shortened, no flesh would be saved; but for the elect's sake those days will be shortened. Matthew 24:21-22

Nothing since the beginning of the world compares to these last three and a half years. Nothing. Not mankind's great wars, not prophetic birth pangs, or even the first half. Death, destruction and persecution piled on top of more death, destruction and persecution. And the wizardry of science in the blood-soaked hands of the Antichrist contributes heavily to his hold on the world. Having allowed Israel to rebuild their temple so he could defile it, the Antichrist no longer needs to be nice to them. It is during this time that Israel flees from his malevolent grip into a place of safety prepared for her by the Lord. This story is told in two heavenly signs that are described in Revelation 12. The first identifies Israel and the second the Antichrist kingdom seeking her destruction.

> [1] Now a great sign appeared in heaven: a woman clothed with the sun, with the moon under her feet, and on her head a garland of twelve stars. [2] Then being with child, she cried out in labor and in pain to give birth.
>
> [3] And another sign appeared in heaven: behold, a great, fiery red dragon having seven heads and ten horns, and seven diadems on his heads. [4] His tail drew a third of the stars of heaven and threw them to the earth. Revelation 12:1-4

The woman is Israel. She is the one who produced the Christ child. The dragon and his Antichrist kingdom of "seven heads and ten horns" pursue the woman. But he is no match for God who provides a place of safety for the woman (Israel) during the entire last half of the seven years.

> ⁶Then the woman fled into the wilderness, where she has a place prepared by God, that they should feed her there one thousand two hundred and sixty days. Revelation 12:6

Revelation 12 tells that Israel is brought to a place of safety. In the meantime, in heaven a great battle is raging. It is an angelic battle pitting the dragon against "Michael and his angels." The result is that the dragon is cast down to the earth. "Having great wrath, because he knows that he has a short time." The Lord's protection of Israel enrages the dragon. As a result "he went to make war with the rest of her offspring, who keep the commandments of God and have the testimony of Jesus Christ." A time of hellish persecution gurgles up from the pit and spreads out across the entire earth against Christians. While at the same time, God protects the Jews. And there is a good reason for this difference in treatment.

Those who have accepted Christ are already saved and will go directly to heaven upon being martyred. And in their deaths, God is glorified because "they loved not their lives unto death" as Revelation 11 tells us. Those believers receive eternal rewards for their faithfulness unto death. Whereas the Jews have not yet accepted Christ. But due to the hundred and forty-four thousand witnessing to their fellow Jews, their acceptance of the Savior is progressive during the second half culminating with the entire nation of Israel being saved at its end. Should they die before coming to Him they would go directly to hell for rejecting the Savior — still drenched in a lifetime of sin. The fact that Christians are being brutally persecuted as Jews are being protected runs hard against some teachings. But the verses are unambiguous in telling us exactly that.

Meanwhile, as Christians are severely persecuted and Israel has fled into God's protective custody other spiritually unique events are unfolding. After desecrating the rebuilt holy Jewish temple by sitting in it and declaring himself a god, the wicked one requires every person on earth to join in his demonic delusion.

> [4] So they worshiped the dragon who gave authority to the beast; and they worshiped the beast, saying, "Who is like the beast? Who is able to make war with him?" Revelation 13:4

For the entire second half of the seven-year tribulation — after the Antichrist defiles the holy temple — deceived minions across the planet worship the dragon — Satan. It is the ultimate deception. He is having his day. They also fall down before the beast in worship. As they do so the Antichrist is opening "his mouth in blasphemy against God, to blaspheme His name, His tabernacle, and those who dwell in heaven." He is even granted authority to test the saints in both patience and faith.

> [7] It was granted to him to make war with the saints and to overcome them. And authority was given him over every tribe, tongue, and nation. [8] All who dwell on the earth will worship him, whose names have not been written in the Book of Life of the Lamb slain from the foundation of the world. Revelation 13:7-8

Not only does severe persecution rain down upon Christians, but they are literally having warfare directed against them by the dark one. And they are "overcome" by these assaults. As resistance against the beast kingdom begins to crumble, and the entire world is given over to him, the legions of the lost worship the beast. A diabolical act of eternal damnation. But not the children of God. Their names are written in the Book of Life. They follow "the Lamb slain from the foundation of the world" unto death. Glorifying their Father in Heaven and themselves receiving eternal rewards.

As the beast dominates the world stage and is its most powerful political leader another wicked figure stands by his side. He is a false religious leader who is also called a beast and a false prophet. He is capable of performing "great signs so that he even makes fire come down from heaven on the earth in the sight of men. [14] And he deceives those who dwell on the earth by those signs which he was granted to do in the sight of the beast, telling those who dwell on the earth to make an image to the beast who was wounded by the sword and lived."

The goal of this second beast is to cause "the earth and those who dwell in it to worship the first beast, whose deadly wound was healed" — damning their souls for all eternity. In addition to possessing the awesome power to make "fire come down from heaven on the earth in the sight of men," he can do something else that is very strange. Even freakish.

There is a statute of the Antichrist. Perhaps it is one that famously celebrates his resurrection back to life after "his deadly wound was healed." It is destined to become the most famous statute in world history. Before a stunned world, the false prophet is "granted power to give breath to the image of the beast, that the image of the beast should both speak and cause as many as would not worship the image of the beast to be killed." It is the most spine-tingling moment in human history. Driving talons of demonic influence ever deeper into the minds of the unsaved.

Just as the Lord places a seal on the forehead of His followers the dragon has his own mark. And he requires it to be placed on the foreheads or the right hand of all people. It is a sign of allegiance to the beast and all people, regardless of rank, "both small and great, rich and poor, free and slave, to receive a mark on their right hand or on their foreheads." There is great pressure to take this passport to hell. Because "no one may buy or sell except one who has the mark or the name of the beast, or the number of his name."

This mark has a unique characteristic associated with it. It is intimately identified with the beast. Scripture tells us it is "the mark or the name of the beast, or the number of his name. [18] Here is wisdom. Let him who has understanding calculate the number of the beast, for it is the number of a man: His number is 666."

As the pages of Revelation turn to chapter fourteen the one hundred and forty-four thousand servants from the twelve tribes have concluded their ministry. And it has had a profound impact. Israel is primed to accept Jesus. Now these faithful servants find themselves singing before the throne of God in heaven. Exactly when they get there within the last half of the seven years we are not told. But they are there and singing a song no one else in heaven can learn. Not even the elders.

In a startling admission, we are told: "the one hundred and forty-four thousand servants... were redeemed from among men, being firstfruits to God and to the Lamb." Do they not taste death? And "firstfruits" of what harvest? (This is addressed in Chapter Eleven "The Resurrection of the Dead and Rapture") Now the next angel appears to announce something new. And its implications are staggering.

> [6] Then I saw another angel flying in the midst of heaven, having the everlasting gospel to preach to those who dwell on the earth—to every nation, tribe, tongue, and people— [7] saying with a loud voice, "Fear God and give glory to Him, for the hour of His judgment has come; and worship Him who made heaven and earth, the sea and springs of water." Revelation 14:6-7

Throughout the long history of the church the gospel has never been preached to the whole world. Until now. It was Jesus on the Mount of Olives who said "this gospel of the kingdom will be preached in all the world as a witness to all the nations, and then the end will come." He was talking about the end of the (church) age. Now an angel has finally done it. (Its significance is dealt with in Chapter Eleven "The Resurrection of the Dead and the Rapture") The next angel appears to make a new announcement. He calls out a city named Babylon.

> [8] And another angel followed, saying, "Babylon is fallen,
> is fallen, that great city, because she has made all nations drink of the wine of the wrath of her fornication."
> Revelation 14:8

This foul and odious city Babylon is soaked in the blood of the martyrs. Revelation 17-18 covers it in depth. It is a city destined to be devoured by its own. But not until it sews a harvest of barbarous destruction across the globe. Its identity is shrouded in mystery. Is it Rome? Is it Mecca? Or is it some other city? It is referred to as yet another beast aligned with the Antichrist. Beasts abound at this time. It is also described as a harlot and for good reason. It is riding the beast kingdom which is its john. Her other johns are the kings of the earth. Many have defiled themselves with her. And like many expensive prostitutes she is well dressed "arrayed in purple and scarlet, and adorned with gold and precious stones and pearls." She is and has been a plague to Christians — her seamy hands dripping "with the blood of the martyrs of Jesus." Her downfall comes at the hands of those within her own camp.

Like Jack the Ripper so turn the *ten kings* against this whore. They "hate the harlot, make her desolate and naked, eat her flesh and burn her with fire." But they unwittingly do the work of God because "her sins have reached to heaven and God has remembered her iniquities." When they are finished with her she becomes "a dwelling place of demons, a prison for every foul spirit, and a cage for every unclean and hated bird!" She is done. The next angel appears. And his is a dire warning of eternal danger.

After sitting in the rebuilt Jewish temple the Antichrist has forced mankind to worship him as a god. And the reason why is beastly. "If anyone worships the beast and his image, and receives his mark on his forehead or on his hand, ¹⁰ he himself shall also drink of the wine of the wrath of God." But the Lord's wrath against those who take the mark extends beyond this world. They "shall be tormented with fire and brimstone in the presence of the holy angels and in the presence of the Lamb. ¹¹ And the smoke of their torment ascends forever and ever; and they have no rest day or night, who worship the beast and his image, and whoever receives the mark of his name." The devil gets their souls for all eternity.

Out from the temple in heaven comes another angel. The moment the church has been longing for has finally arrived. "One like the Son of Man" appears sitting on a "white cloud." It is Jesus. This new announcing angel cries "with a loud voice to Him who sat on the cloud, "Thrust in Your sickle and reap, for the time has come for You to reap, for the harvest of the earth is ripe." So He who sat on the cloud thrust in His sickle on the earth, and the earth was reaped." The "harvest of the earth" was just reaped. (This is explained in Chapter Eleven "The Resurrection of the Dead and the Rapture") Although brief in description this appearance of Jesus in the clouds is a great blessing. And it is not to be blended with the next and final event about to be described.

Now appears the last announcing angel to describe the next and final event given to us in Revelation 14. Announcing angels are used in this chapter to distinguish and keep separate each of the six events described therein. Each event in the chapter has the appearance of a new announcing angel. The observable structure of Revelation 14 is the use of announcing angels to keep separate the six events described in the chapter all of which unfold during the second half of the seven years. These are all broad overviews. That is all this chapter does. An overview of certain second-half events. That's all. And the use of announcing angels is to prevent the reader from blending these events. This Divine design keeps separate the event of Jesus taking His harvest from this last event described which includes much blood.

Another angel comes "out of the temple which is in heaven." And his appearance tells us another event is about to be described. He too holds a "sickle." But he will reap a very different crop than the harvest the Son of Man just took. It is grapes of wrath he seeks. Then an angel possessing "power over fire" joins him in this grim task. The grapes of the earth are cut down with the swing of his angelic hand. They are thrown "into the great winepress of the wrath of God." This same phrase, "winepress of the fierceness and wrath of Almighty God," is also used in describing the Battle of Armageddon in both Revelation 19 and Joel 3.

The six events and admonitions described in Revelation 14 are major ones (Not all-inclusive) covering the last half of the seven years. The six are:

- The completion of the ministry of the one hundred and forty-four thousand.
- The preaching of the gospel to the entire world.
- The fall of mystery Babylon.
- Admonitions against worshiping the beast.
- The coming of the Son of Man with His sickle to take His harvest.
- And the Battle of Armageddon.

Each is kept separate by a new announcing angel. But those descriptions of the six events unfolding across the second half of the seven years are as a layer of icing over a cake of seven plagues unfolding concurrently with them.

In announcing the seven bowl judgments that will unfold across the final half of the seven years there is one word that stands out. Last. And this means they cannot be a repeat of the trumpet judgments as some try to say. Some of their descriptions are similar to the trumpet judgments, but they are distinctly much more severe and again stress that they are different from the trumpets. We are told the "Seven angels having the seven last plagues" now appear on the scene. As they do the temple in heaven is "filled with smoke from the glory of God and from His power," and no one is allowed to enter the temple until the angels have completed their brutal task on the earth.

As the first bowl is unleashed so too are foul and loathsome sores. But only upon those "men who had the mark of the beast and those who worshiped his image." Those who are still alive who have not taken the mark of the beast or worshiped his image are free from this plague. They are believers and it is impossible for the Lord's wrath to touch them. And this protection represents a piercing physiological thorn in the side of the followers of the Antichrist. The second bowl is poured forth.

When it is released mankind suffers the defilement of the seas. The same defilement that was inflicted a few years earlier by the second trumpeter. But it is much worse this time. That second trumpeter caused only a "third of the sea" to be turned to blood and the death of "a third of the living creatures" in it. Now every drop of ocean water is blood and "every living creature in the sea" dies.

Since the savage and heartless followers of the Antichrist have hands dripping with "the blood of saints and prophets," the perfect justice of God dictates blood be their drink. With all sea water made blood his demented followers seek water inland. But to no avail. As the third angel "pours out his bowl on the rivers and springs of water" they too become blood. It is the same plague the Lord used to get the attention of the ancient Egyptians.

The darkened minds of the followers of the Antichrist are completely crazed now. Embracing a false god and terrorizing followers of the True One their minds are ravaged. As the fourth bowl is poured forth the sun begins scorching them with fire and great heat. But instead of repenting their twisted minds lead them to blaspheme God and they do "not re-pent and give Him glory." They are hopelessly evil now.

As in the time of ancient Egypt the Lord once again brings darkness to a kingdom defying Him. This time it unfolds over the darkest kingdom the world will ever know. As "the fifth angel poured out his bowl on the throne of the beast, and his kingdom became full of darkness." And his blood-thirsty followers "gnawed their tongues because of the pain." Still they "did not repent of their deeds."

Wars

The day of the Lord (end times) has several devastating wars within it. In the beginning, the fiery red horse of the apocalypse brought with him war. A great war including the use of nuclear weapons according to 2 Peter 3:10, wherein we are told "the heavens will pass away with a great noise, and the elements will melt with fervent heat, both the earth and the works that are in it will be burned up." Following that war, the black and pale horses unleash great famine, pestilence, and disease, as well as the sword. And these wars are only the birth pangs beginning of the day of the Lord. Following those wars during the first half of the seven years, the trumpet of the sixth angel unleashes "four angels who are bound at the great river Euphrates." Their mission is staggering. "So the four angels, who had been prepared for the hour and day and month and year, were released to kill a third of mankind." And they accomplish it by unleashing strange horse-men numbering two hundred million. These horsemen bring with them fire, smoke, and brimstone to accomplish their grisly task. But as bad as these wars have been there is yet another to come.

It has been said that only the dead have seen the end of war. And soon the ranks of those who will see no more war are about to swell. As the *sixth angel* prepares to pour out his horrific bowl the final war of the end times approaches and with it the world's most famous battle.

CHAPTER TEN

The Battles of Armageddon, Judah & Jerusalem

The pages of history are littered with famous battles. Conflicts that determined the fate of millions of people. Napoleon's defeat at the Battle of Waterloo ensured Europe would not be ruled by a single tyrant — much to the delight of the ones already there. And if Hitler's efforts to defeat Great Britain at the Battle of Britain had succeeded, then Britain's "finest hour" would have morphed into her darkest, swinging the hinge of European history from freedom to abject slavery. In American history, it was the Battle at Yorktown that resulted in the birth of the most powerful political and military force the world has ever known — America. But there is another battle the prophets tell us is coming. One that will determine the fate of the entire world for a thousand years.

The pouring of the sixth bowl clears the way for the greatest battle of all time. The Battle of Armageddon. It is the world's most famous battle that is yet to be fought. Now its day has arrived. The bowl dries up "the great river Euphrates" removing it as a natural barrier. Great armies destined across time to meet in this battle have begun gathering.

Revelation 19 finds the army of heaven being led by Jesus. He is riding a white horse to battle. "And the armies in heaven, clothed in fine linen, white and clean, followed Him on white horses." The children of God are

His army. And within their ranks are those with a score to settle. They are the ones who suffered butchery at the hands of the Antichrist and his followers. Joining them are martyrs across the ages. Revelation 6 tells of these martyrs gathered "under the altar" in heaven. It is a place of honor. Each is given a white robe to wear. They are told to wait for the time of vengeance to arrive. They want their blood avenged! And their Father is more than willing to do so. Their wait is over. As the eyes of every living being in heaven look on as the day of the great battle has arrived. On the other side facing the army of God are the forces of darkness. And they have assembled the greatest army the world has ever seen.

With the raging river Euphrates dried up the way is made to Armageddon for "the kings from the east." But the ten kings, beholden to the Antichrist for their kingdoms, they and their armies are called to this battle in another way. By demonic signs. And it is a foul and odious call. Where "three unclean spirits like frogs come out of the mouth of the dragon, out of the mouth of the beast, and out of the mouth of the false prophet." The power of these spirits is of performing signs. And these signs draw "the kings of the earth and of the whole world, to gather them to the battle of that great day of God Almighty." They are impressed by these supernatural signs and likely see them as an omen of certain victory. Anointed and appointed by the Antichrist to rule the conquered lands they form ranks behind him. In league with him are his detestable allies: the lion, leopard, and bear. Although these kings of the earth are gathered for the greatest battle in world history the outcome is never in doubt.

Armageddon represents the winepress of the fierceness and wrath of Almighty God. These grapes of wrath are punishment against all nations for their wickedness. This is the same grapes of wrath phrase used by John in the last of the six events listed in Revelation 14 to identify Armageddon. It is also used in Revelation 19. Joel uses it in chapter 3 for the Battle of Armageddon in his second reference to the Valley of Jehoshaphat. (The first reference in Joel is to the initial punishment against all nations for parting the land of Israel and launching the day of the Lord.) But as the Battle of Armageddon rages other great battles unfold along with it.

Battles of Judah & Jerusalem

Zechariah 12 & 14 has much to say about these battles. As the Lord and His forces do battle on the "plain of Megiddo, Judah will be besieged as well as Jerusalem." But Judah is not experiencing the same degree of destruction as Jerusalem. And that is likely because the main goal of the Antichrist is to retake the holy temple in Jerusalem. With the forces of the Antichrist attacking Jerusalem en masse, the city's defenses are buckling. But before rescuing Jerusalem from the fury of attacking hordes, Judah is where the Lord's attention first turns. "I will keep a watchful eye over Judah." And there is a Divine reason for this choice.

> "The LORD will save the dwellings of Judah first, so that the honor of the house of David and of Jerusalem's inhabitants may not be greater than that of Judah. Zechariah 12:7

The Lord's intervention in the battle is supernatural. He "blind[s] all the horses of the nations" attacking Judah. The people of Judah recognize their deliverance was Divine. It is obvious. But they also know Jerusalem is under a violent and devastating siege. Having just experienced the Lord's supernatural deliverance from overwhelming odds, the people of Judah now turn their attention to Jerusalem. It is the ancient city of their fathers and the focal point of their faith. And they "say in their hearts, 'The people of Jerusalem are strong, because the LORD Almighty is their God.'"

After delivering Judah from the fury of Antichrist the condition of Jerusalem worsens by the moment. The great city is being "plundered and divided up within [its] very walls." Within the captured sections of the city "houses [are] ransacked, and the women raped. Half of the city will go into exile, but the rest of the people will not be taken from the city." The city is being ravaged. But the entire city has not yet fallen. And for good reason.

> [8] On that day the LORD will shield those who live in Jerusalem, so that the feeblest among them will be like David, and the house of David will be like God, like the angel of the LORD going before them. Zechariah 12:8

Those fighting to protect Jerusalem are supernaturally empowered by God. Although greatly outnumbered by the swarming fighters of the Antichrist they become mighty warriors. As for Judah since being delivered by the Lord from the attacking army of the Antichrist both victory and safety have come to them. But not rest. The people of Judah now turn their gaze toward their brothers fighting at Jerusalem. "Judah too will fight at Jerusalem." But Judah is not alone. "Then the LORD will go out and fight against those nations, as he fights on a day of battle." The Lord has joined the battle for Jerusalem. "On that day I will set out to destroy all the nations that attack Jerusalem." The One who "lays the foundation of the earth, and who forms the human spirit within a person, declares:"

> [2] "I am going to make Jerusalem a cup that sends all the surrounding peoples reeling. Judah will be besieged as well as Jerusalem. [3] On that day, when all the nations of the earth are gathered against her, I will make Jerusalem an immovable rock for all the nations. All who try to move it will injure themselves. [4] On that day I will strike every horse with panic and its rider with madness," declares the LORD. Zechariah 12:2-4

The assault of the Lord against the legions of the Antichrist attacking Jerusalem is devastating. He strikes them with a plague that "their flesh will rot while they are still standing on their feet, their eyes will rot in their sockets, and their tongues will rot in their mouths." But He is not finished.

For those not stricken with that horror, a different one awaits. "On that day people will be stricken by the LORD with great panic. They will seize each other by the hand and attack one another." He afflicts their already tormented minds with a form of madness causing each to turn on the other. And as these great battles unfold so too does a great supernatural event.

The Lord of Hosts — the God of Abraham, Isaac, and Jacob — who has hidden His face from sinful man since the fall now comes out in full view for all to see. And it is glorious. He enters the battle as that of a conquering king.

> [11] Now I saw heaven opened, and behold, a white horse. And He who sat on him was called Faithful and True, and in righteousness He judges and makes war. [12] His eyes were like a flame of fire, and on His head were many crowns. He had a name written that no one knew except Himself. [13] He was clothed with a robe dipped in blood, and His name is called The Word of God. Revelation 19

It is the Lord. He has come to do battle with eyes "like a flame of fire" and riding a white horse. The weapon He wields against the wicked nations is a uniquely powerful one. "Now out of His mouth goes a sharp sword, that with it He should strike the nations." His entry into the world ultimately takes Him to the city of Jerusalem. He descends to the ground. And once again His feet stand on the Mount of Olives. The last time this happened was during His earthly ministry. Now He has returned just as He said He would.

> [4] On that day his feet will stand on the Mount of Olives east of Jerusalem, and the Mount of Olives will be split in two from east to west, forming a great valley, with half of the mountain moving north and half moving south. Zechariah 14

Understandably, the mountain splits in two when His feet touch it. These are the feet of God Himself. Not only are the modern Israelites staggered by the visible reality of the Lord coming to rescue them — against impossible odds as in the olden days — but along with this salvation comes a devastating realization. Being able to now clearly see the One they call their God, they see something else as well.

> [10]They will look on me, the one they have pierced, and they will mourn for him as one mourns for an only child, and grieve bitterly for him as one grieves for a first-born son. [11]On that day the weeping in Jerusalem will be as great as the weeping of Hadad Rimmon in the plain of Megiddo. Zechariah 12

It is a reality denied by Jews for generations. They killed their Messiah. Now realizing their error they turn to Him in the fullness of hearts wracked with grief and weeping. Meanwhile, on the other side of the battle, Isaiah describes events engulfing Antichrist and his princes. As it becomes clear to the Antichrist that defeat is near his kingly robe is replaced with a cloak of shame.

> [8]Then shall the <u>Assyrian</u> fall with the sword, not of a mighty man; and the sword, not of a mean man, shall devour him: but he shall flee from the sword, and his young men shall be discomfited. [9]And he shall pass over to his strong hold for fear, and his <u>princes</u> shall be afraid of the ensign, (BANNER) saith the LORD, whose fire is in Zion, and his furnace in Jerusalem. Isaiah 31

The "Assyrian" also known as Antichrist is humiliated. Instead of fighting to the death — a fitting end for a king — "he shall flee from the sword" like a coward bringing great discomfort to the young men who foolishly followed him. And his princes seeing destruction unfold all about, as well as their leader fleeing, now fear the battle flag of the Lord's army. The prophet Isaiah foretold the end of the Assyrian who is also called the beast in scripture and called the Antichrist by men. He has many names.

> The LORD of hosts has sworn, saying, "Surely, as I have thought, so it shall come to pass, And as I have purposed, so it shall stand: 25 That I will break the Assyrian in My land, And on My mountains tread him underfoot. Then his yoke shall be removed from them, And his burden removed from their shoulders. 26 This is the purpose that is purposed against the whole earth, And this is the hand that is stretched out over all the nations. Isaiah 14

Daniel 8 sees "the beast was slain, and its body destroyed and given to the burning flame." As for his three major allies known as "the rest of the beasts, they had their dominion taken away, yet their lives were prolonged for a season and a time." He is referring to the lion, leopard, and bear the three major nations that followed Antichrist to destruction. John adds more detail in Revelation 19.

He notes "the beast was captured, and with him the false prophet who worked signs in his presence, by which he deceived those who received the mark of the beast and those who worshiped his image." Like Daniel his fellow prophet John sees the Antichrist and false prophet suffer fire. They are "cast alive into the lake of fire burning with brimstone." As for the ten kings, their flesh becomes a feast for the birds of the air. And when the battle is finished only birds heavy laden with the remains of kings are left.

In the aftermath of victory, the condition of the world dramatically changes. It is a new day celebrated with singing from those who were oppressed.

> 4"How the oppressor has ceased, The golden city ceased!
> 5 The LORD has broken the staff of the wicked, The scepter
> of the rulers; 6 He who struck the people in wrath with a

continual stroke, He who ruled the nations in anger, Is persecuted and no one hinders. [7] The whole earth is at rest and quiet; They break forth into singing. Isaiah 14

The Antichrist has suffered a complete defeat at the hands of the Lord and is finally dead to this world. As the people of the earth "break forth into singing" for finally being rid of the beast and his beastly allies, those in the next world await his arrival with glee in the most spine-chilling welcome ever.

The Greeting of Hell

In the underworld, the doomed await the arrival of the Antichrist to offer their morbid welcome. Condemned souls wanting more souls to join their terrifying and never-ending fate in the winding caverns of hell. It is the most grotesque greeting ever. Hell's current occupants — distorted and twisted from countless years in fire and brimstone — are apparently aware of events transpiring on the earth. They know their ranks will soon be joined by the Antichrist. They are excited and prepare a proper greeting for the one who shook the world.

> [9]"Hell from beneath is excited about you, To meet you at your coming;
> It stirs up the dead for you, All the chief ones of the earth;
> It has raised up from their thrones All the kings of the nations. Isaiah 14

The dead of hell — ghoulish and grisly in appearance — are aroused to the knowledge of who is about to join their macabre ranks. Their excitement is so great that they stir up among themselves the most important ones. "The chief ones" and "all the kings of the nations" whose eternal home became fire, darkness and pain. They gather together forming its dreadful greeting party. And in dark fashion upon his arrival, they mock him saying: "'Is this the man who made the earth tremble, Who shook kingdoms, Who made the world as a wilderness And destroyed its cities, Who did not open the house of his prisoners?'" They taunt him and compare him to the glory of previous kings.

> [18] "All the kings of the nations, All of them, sleep in glory, Everyone in his own house; [19] But you are cast out of your grave Like an abominable branch, Like the garment of those who are slain, Thrust through with a sword, Who go down to the stones of the pit, Like a corpse trodden underfoot. [20] You will not be joined with them in burial, Because you have destroyed your land And slain your people. Isaiah 14

Once the most powerful man to ever live — greater than Caesar, Napoleon, or Hitler — the occupants of hell say to the Antichrist: "'Have you also become as weak as we? Have you become like us? [11] Your pomp is brought down to Sheol, and the sound of your stringed instruments." The Antichrist has made himself a bed in hell. His ghastly body doomed to rest on a mattress of "the maggot." Covered by a blanket of "worms" for all eternity according to Isaiah 14. His fate is sealed.

Why is Armageddon Necessary?

With the Antichrist relegated to Sheol after losing the battles of Armageddon, Judah and Jerusalem, the question arises as to why it is necessary for him to fight those battles in the first place. That question presents itself because only three and a half years earlier he possessed the City of Jerusalem and the temple. We know this because he abominates the temple at the midpoint and the Jews are unable to stop him. And the reason why they could not stop him is spelled out in Daniel 8.

[11] He even exalted himself as high as the Prince of the host; and by him the daily sacrifices were taken away, and the place of His sanctuary was cast down. [12] Because of transgression, an army was given over to the horn to oppose the daily sacrifices; and he cast truth down to the ground. He did all this and prospered. Daniel 8

We are told that due to "transgression an army was given over to the horn (Antichrist) to oppose the daily sacrifices" and to defile the temple. This is why he is able to control Jerusalem and defile the temple at the midpoint of the seven years. He has an occupying army there. But it is also clear that sometime within the second half of the seven years his army loses control of the city. By the time the Battle of Armageddon takes place, instead of controlling Jerusalem, the Antichrist must attack the city to retake it. But clearly sometime after the midpoint, but prior to Armageddon, the Jews retake the city making it necessary for Antichrist to launch the massive invasion that results in those battles. Does the Lord supernaturally enable Israel to take back the holy city and the temple? Thus creating irresistible bait to draw Antichrist and his beast armies to their destruction at Armageddon? It would appear so since the Lord is in control. Now the question arises as to how many days before Armageddon do the Jews retake the holy city? And there is reason to believe it will be one hundred and ten days. Here is why that may be the time frame. This is speculation and you must decide if it makes sense.

We know the last half of the seven years is 1260 days. The Lord speaks of this time frame in several different ways. In Revelation 12:6 He directly says "one thousand two hundred and sixty days." Later in the chapter He describes it "as a time and times and half a time." In Revelation 13:5 He describes it as "forty-two months." For whatever reason He likes using different ways of expressing the same time frame. Remember that. Now consider Daniel 8 where we are told how many days will pass from the mid-point — when Antichrist begins defiling the temple — until the temple is finally cleansed of the wicked one's presence and all his defilements within it. And for the temple to be cleansed the Israelites will first have to drive the forces of Antichrist out of the City of Jerusalem.

> [13] Then I heard a holy one speaking; and another holy one said to that certain one who was speaking, "How long will the vision be, concerning the daily sacrifices and the transgression of desolation, the giving of both the sanctuary and the host to be trampled underfoot?"
>
> [14] And he said to me, "For two thousand three hundred days; then the sanctuary shall be cleansed."

We are told that from the time Antichrist sits in the temple defiling it until the time it is no longer being "trampled underfoot" by him will be "two thousand three hundred days." And this information immediately creates impossible math. How can it take 2300 days to put an end to the temple being trampled underfoot by Antichrist, when there are only 1260 days remaining in his rule? Those 1260 days are from the midpoint until the Battle of Armageddon after which he is immediately sent to Sheol. Since on the 1260th day, he meets his eternal fate at Armageddon, how can the temple continue to be "trampled underfoot" by him after that? And, of course, the answer is he cannot continue to do so. Those residing in Sheol no longer have the power to trample anything on the earth. So the "two thousand three hundred days" creates a serious conflict in time frames. However, the solution to this puzzling number may rest in the unique way in which those 2300 days are being described.

Throughout the Old Testament Bible, the word used for day is the Hebrew masculine noun "yom." In fact, it is used over two thousand times. Most of the time it is used for a 24-hour period. But sometimes it is used for a span of time such as in the phrase the day of the Lord. In the Book of Daniel "yom" is used 23 times. However, in Daniel 8:14 when speaking about the two thousand three hundred days something very different is done for the word days in that verse. Uniquely, two Hebrew words are used there to describe those days. And both of them mean only a portion of a day. The first is "Ereb" meaning evenings or nights and the second is "boqeu" meaning mornings. "Yom" is not found there. Because of this in Strong's Concordance two separate Hebrew footnotes are provided for that single word day. And that is highly unusual being the only place in Daniel, and possibly in the entire Bible, where this is done concerning the word day. So the Lord is doing something very different here in describing these specific 2300 days.

Speculation

Since two thousand three hundred days create the impossible math previously mentioned, what the Lord may be doing here is telling us that the combined number of evenings and mornings will equal 2300. We already know He likes to present time frames in different ways having done so in three different ways to describe the 1260 days. And if this is the case then it translates into 1150 actual 24-hour days until the "sanctuary shall be cleansed" from the time Antichrist begins defiling it at the mid-point. If this is the case then it eliminates the impossible math and indicates that the Jews will retake the City of Jerusalem 1150 days into the second half leaving only 110 days remaining until Armageddon. The Jews retaking Jerusalem 110 days before the end times conclude would not only provide the reason Antichrist goes to war to retake the city and the temple, but will also give him 110 days to gather his armies for the invasion. Since the Battle of Armageddon, Judah and Jerusalem happen on the 1260th day — at the end of the second half — then the Jews retaking the city and temple would take place 110 days prior to that battle if this perspective is correct.

The Seventh Bowl

After His two witnesses were resurrected and brought back to heaven the Lord used a great earthquake as His exclamation point to their ministry. Now with the battles of Armageddon, Judah and Jerusalem finished He does so again. But the earthquake unleashed here dwarfs the previous one. After the seventh angel pours his bowl he issues forth a statement that rings about in the heavens. "It is done!" The seventieth week of Daniel, also known as the seven-year tribulation, is finally complete.

The earthquake set forth in this final act of the Lord's wrath causes Jerusalem to be "divided into three parts, and the cities of the nations fell." Islands and mountains are altered with some no longer found. And enormous hail rains down on men. Now there is only one remaining act of justice to be done.

Dealing with the Devil

Satan, also known as the dragon and the devil has brought utter destruction to mankind. His specialty is deception. And he has employed it with staggering skill since the time Adam met Eve. His horrid turn from light to darkness happened in a moment. The sin of pride entered the one "full of wisdom and perfect in beauty." His fall was seeking the throne of God for himself. An absurdity damning him for all eternity. Yet, before his fall the Lord had been generous to him beyond measure. In vivid terms, Ezekiel 28 speaks to this generosity.

> ...Thus says the Lord GOD:
> "You were the seal of perfection,
> Full of wisdom and perfect in beauty.
> [13] You were in Eden, the garden of God;
> Every precious stone was your covering:
> The sardius, topaz, and diamond,

Beryl, onyx, and jasper,
Sapphire, turquoise, and emerald with gold.
The workmanship of your timbrels and pipes
Was prepared for you on the day you were created.
¹⁴ "You were the anointed cherub who covers;
I established you;
You were on the holy mountain of God;
You walked back and forth in the midst of fiery stones.

And then it happened. He fell.

¹⁵ You were perfect in your ways from the day you were created,
Till iniquity was found in you.
¹⁶ "By the abundance of your trading
You became filled with violence within,
And you sinned;
Therefore I cast you as a profane thing
Out of the mountain of God;
And I destroyed you, O covering cherub,
From the midst of the fiery stones.
¹⁷ "Your heart was lifted up because of your beauty;
You corrupted your wisdom for the sake of your splendor;
I cast you to the ground,
I laid you before kings,
That they might gaze at you.
¹⁸ "You defiled your sanctuaries
By the multitude of your iniquities,
By the iniquity of your trading;
Therefore I brought fire from your midst;
It devoured you,
And I turned you to ashes upon the earth

In the sight of all who saw you.
¹⁹ All who knew you among the peoples are astonished at you;
You have become a horror,
And shall be no more forever." '"

An astonishing fall from *beauty* and perfection. In fact, it was due to his *beauty* that "his heart was lifted up." And his "wisdom" was corrupted for the sake of his "splendor." His rebellion started a war against God that he could never win. So he turned his wrath against those he could defeat. Mankind. Now having been cast out of heaven by Michael and his angels, and with his earthly army defeated at the Battle of Armageddon, his devastating run against mankind has come to an end. But only for a thousand years as he suffers the fate of the bottomless pit — a Divine holding tank.

It is a powerful angel from heaven who brings him there. But first, the angel binds him with "a great chain" — one destined to spend a "thousand years" on his hulking body. His mouth is shut. He can no longer deceive by wicked utterings. Set upon him is a "seal." Seals from God are unbreakable. The judgment of God is that he spend a thousand years in its black depths. Isaiah speaks of his fall.

> ¹² "How you are fallen from heaven, O Lucifer, son of the morning!
> How you are cut down to the ground, You who weakened the nations!
> ¹³ For you have said in your heart: 'I will ascend into heaven,
> I will exalt my throne above the stars of God; I will also sit on the mount of the congregation On the farthest sides of the north; ¹⁴ I will ascend above the heights of the clouds, I will be like the Most High.' ¹⁵ Yet you shall be brought down to Sheol, To the lowest depths of the Pit. Isaiah 14

The Pit Satan has entered is the same one Apollyon came out of as the fifth angel of Revelation sounded his trumpet. It was at that time "that a star fallen from heaven to the earth. To him was given the key to the bottomless pit. [2]And he opened the bottomless pit, and smoke arose out of the pit like the smoke of a great furnace. So the sun and the air were darkened because of the smoke of the pit."

The lowest depths of "pit of smoke" are now his home. But only for those thousand years will he be trapped within its confines. Thereafter he is set loose finding terrible success once more against his hated enemy — mankind. And he uses his freedom to deceive the nations into invading Israel again in an apparent replay of Armageddon. Making it clear the thoughts that will possess his mind during those thousand years in the pit.

> [7]Now when the thousand years have expired, Satan will be released from his prison [8]and will go out to deceive the nations which are in the four corners of the earth, Gog and Magog, to gather them together to battle, whose number is as the sand of the sea. [9]They went up on the breadth of the earth and surrounded the camp of the saints and the beloved city. And fire came down from God out of heaven and devoured them. Revelation 20

After a thousand years of peace, mankind will be deceived by the evil one yet again. A sad testimony to the nature of fallen man. The nations attacking Israel are gathered under the banner of "Gog and Magog." Although their number is as great "as the sand of the sea" they are swiftly dealt with by fire. The Lord is the God of Israel. The battle is over. The enemy is defeated once again just as he was at Armageddon. The Lord is now finished with Satan. From the start, his horrid existence was used to demonstrate the glory and goodness of the Holy One. Now eternal judgment comes to the wicked one. The "lake of fire" will be his abode "forever and ever" time without end.

[10] The devil, who deceived them, was cast into the lake of fire and brimstone where the beast and the false prophet are. And they will be tormented day and night forever and ever. Revelation 20

The Gog Magog War

That the devil seeks a replay of Armageddon after the thousand-years have passed is not surprising. He has had much time to ponder it. Revelation 20 is clear that the wicked one uses Gog and Magog to gather the nations together for the attack against Israel. But there is something strange here. How can mankind be deceived yet again after all that happened during the end times? Especially in light of modern technology allowing supernatural events to be recorded as they happened. And no doubt during the thousand-year reign of Christ videos will endlessly replay those recorded supernatural moments. Such incredible events as the false prophet calling down fire from the sky. The two witnesses rising from the dead. The supernatural destruction of the forces of the Antichrist at the Battle of Armageddon and the appearance of Jesus Christ riding a white horse. All spelled out in Biblical prophecy and all fulfilled to perfection. But in spite of all this hard evidence mankind manages to be deceived again.

We are not told how long after the thousand years this war will happen. We are only told that after a thousand years Satan is allowed to begin deceiving the nations again. But it will likely take him a length of time before he is able to overcome all of the evidence pointing to the reality of the end times and its perfect fulfillment of Bible prophecy. Including the thousand-year reign of Christ which ushers in a length of peace on earth unlike any in history and also foretold in scripture. So the process of deceiving will likely take some time.

Since Satan doesn't have any new tricks up his sleeve he will likely use the same methods he has employed with great success today. Such as strategically placing individual men with talent and intellect where they can do the most harm. Men whose minds he has great influence. Using "the lust of the flesh, the lust of the eyes, and the pride of life." This is the same as what we see today leading up to the end times. Like today he will probably use "higher" education and "experts" who eventually break through the walls of "ignorance" to bring the light of "knowledge" back to men. And, of course, all of this will be done by using a form of demonic logic to justify it. Just as in current times.

In addition to Revelation 20, there is one more place in scripture that speaks of a Gog Magog invasion of Israel. That is in the Book of Ezekiel chapters 38 and 39. But unlike John in Revelation 20 who is clear it happens after the thousand year's reign of Christ, Ezekiel's version has no specific time frame given. And this has led some to speculate that there are two Gog Magog wars. One after the thousand years as noted by John, and another before the thousand years begin. This camp of a Gog Magog war before the thousand years begin is itself divided into two camps. One says it happens before the end times begin — and others believe it is a description of the Battle of Armageddon. To help sort out these differences consider the following verses in Ezekiel.

> Ezekiel 38: [10] 'Thus says the Lord GOD: "On that day it shall come to pass that thoughts will arise in your mind, and you will make an evil plan: [11] You will say, 'I will go up against a land of unwalled villages; I will go to a peaceful people, who dwell safely, all of them dwelling without walls, and having neither bars nor gates'— [12] to take plunder and to take booty, to stretch out your hand against the waste places that are again inhabited, and against a people gathered from the nations, who have acquired livestock and goods, who dwell in the midst of the land. [13] Sheba, Dedan, the merchants of Tarshish, and all their young lions will say to you, 'Have you come to

> take plunder? Have you gathered your army to take booty,
> to carry away silver and gold, to take away livestock and
> goods, to take great plunder?' "'

We are told that the mind of Gog will begin to contemplate invading Israel. Ezekiel shows us the actual reasoning Gog will use as the justification to invade. And it is quite revealing as to the security condition of Israel at the time this war will take place. Israel is "a land of unwalled villages ... a peaceful people, who dwell safely, all of them dwelling without walls, and having neither bars nor gates'." When the Gog Magog War takes place Israel is a nation without the fences and walls. Ezekiel also tells us it is a nation living "peaceful" and "safely." Consider the three notable characteristics of Israel listed by Ezekiel in those few verses:

1. No fences or walls dividing Israel from her neighbors.
2. They are in a state of peace.
3. They dwell safely.
4. All of which implies no military.

The Problem with Two Gog-Magog Wars

The proponents of an earlier Gog-Magog war have a significant problem to overcome. Those saying Israel could suffer the Gog-Magog invasion any day now typically have the nations of Russia, Iran and Turkey as invading Israel before the end times begin. The first problem with this theory is the present-day condition of Israel. The Jewish state is surrounded by the most formidable fences and walls in the world. And the reason for these barriers is that danger lurks all around them. There is the terrorist organization Hezbollah in Lebanon to the north with its tens of thousands of fighters and rockets aimed at Israel. On the eastern border, there is the Syrian enemy on the other side of the Golan Heights. And at the southern border, there is the terrorist organization Hamas which controls the Gaza region.

So Israel has both walls and fences and is not in a peaceful safe condition. But there is also the realpolitik problem.

From a realpolitik standpoint, Israel has good relations with Russia. In fact, they sell military hardware to them. Additionally, Israel currently has the fifth strongest military in the world including a respectable nuclear weapons arsenal. For any group of nations to even consider invading Israel it would likely take a several million-man army to have any chance against the very large and well-armed Israeli army. And the attacking nations would have to assume that Israel would use her nuclear weapons as she was being destroyed.

Obviously, the perspective that the Gog Magog war could happen any year now is out of line with the realities of present-day Israel. Now consider those who say the Gog-Magog War of Ezekiel 38-39 reflects another perspective on the Battle of Armageddon. But here too there is a problem.

We know from Daniel 8 that at the midpoint of the seven years, Antichrist possesses the City of Jerusalem by way of an army. And he has such a level of control that he is able to sit in and defile the rebuilt Jewish temple. It is also clear that during the last half of the seven years, Israel is under severe persecution from the Antichrist to the point that they will have to flee into the Lord's protective custody according to Revelation 12. We also know that sometime before the Battle of Armageddon Israel is successful in retaking possession of Jerusalem and the holy temple away the Antichrist. And since we are told Antichrist initially took the city by way of an army, then it is reasonable to assume Israel must retake it by the same method. Since Jerusalem and the temple are Satan's end-time focal points, then he is not going to simply allow the Jews to regain control of them without a fight. The Jews retaking Jerusalem is clearly the reason Antichrist will gather his forces for the battles of Judah, Jerusalem and the Battle of Armageddon. He is guided by Satan to retake them. This is the security condition of Israel leading up to the Battle of Armageddon. A condition that in no way resembles the peaceful condition of living safely that Ezekiel describes. So there is a major problem with the theory that Ezekiel's Gog Magog war is another description of the Battle of Armageddon.

However, we do know from Revelation 20 that Gog Magog will invade Israel after a thousand years of peace. During those thousand years, Israel will have no need for walls and fences. Additionally, they will be living peacefully and in complete safety for the first time in their history. For all of these reasons, it appears that Ezekiel's description of the Gog Magog war is simply adding to what John is telling us. And, therefore, there is not a Gog Magog war approaching on the horizon as some try to say.

The Judgment of Men

Across the ages, a plague of evil men has tormented the small and powerless of the world. Men without conscience or feeling ruled with callous disregard for others. They believed their day in the sun would last forever. With the judgment of Satan finished now the Lord turns His attention to the eternal judgment of men. The Holy One has been keeping records. These records span several books documenting the misdeeds of men while on Earth. And contained within these books is nothing less than irrefutable evidence of wickedness. Spiritually recorded to perfection that none can deny. One by one the condemned stand before the throne of God and receive perfect justice.

> [11] Then I saw a great white throne and Him who sat on it, from whose face the earth and the heaven fled away. And there was found no place for them. [12] And I saw the dead, small and great, standing before God, and books were opened. And another book was opened, which is the Book of Life. And the dead were judged according to their works, by the things which were written in the books. Revelation 20

Regardless of where the dead dwell they are brought to judgment. Even "the sea gave up the dead who were in it, and Death and Hades delivered up the dead who were in them. And they were judged, each one according to his works." When judgment is finished they are "cast into the lake of fire. This is the second death." The first death was that of their physical bodies. It is this second death that matters so much more. The lake of fire is the eternal kingdom of Satan. It is this kingdom rebellious men chose while living on the earth. The Lord honors their choice as He will not violate their free will decision.

However, there are also those who took a different route in their earthly life. The narrow road. Their names are found in a different book. The Book of Life. They will spend eternity in the bliss and comfort of heaven while the condemned are tormented in hell. And the pathway into heaven was so easy.

> [16] For God so loved the world that He gave His only begotten Son, that whoever believes in Him should not perish but have everlasting life. [17] For God did not send His Son into the world to condemn the world, but that the world through Him might be saved.
>
> [18] "He who believes in Him is not condemned; but he who does not believe is condemned already, because he has not believed in the name of the only begotten Son of God. [19] And this is the condemnation, that the light has come into the world, and men loved darkness rather than light, because their deeds were evil. John 3:16-19

Rebellious mankind — the breaker one law after another in a Universe created by the perfect and holy God of heaven. Hopelessly facing the consequences of his own black deeds and desperately needing deliverance he cannot grant himself. Such deliverance required a Savior. But unlike whimsical man whose concepts of justice are flawed, the mercy of a perfect

God is limited to the confines of His knowledge of what true justice is. For to do otherwise would relegate Himself to imperfection. As such with the sin of the world needing to be dealt with the perfect justice of God required a payment sufficient to cover that unspeakable debt. Dark sins practiced by billions of people over thousands of years. Uncounted murders, thieveries, adulteries, lies, persecutions, hatreds, deceptions, injustices and others too numerous to be named. In His perfect knowledge, He determined there was only one action within the boundaries of perfect justice capable of fulfilling payment of so colossal a debt. Such vast debt required an infinite payment. This daunting prospect left only one alternative. The saddling of all sin debt on the back of His Holy Son. Receiving His death as payment in full. Since the value of this payment could not be measured, it would be sufficient to wipe clean the slate for mankind. A staggering choice for any father. But the only one capable of fulfilling perfect justice while allowing His mercy to be bestowed upon wayward man.

For those spending eternity in hell the knowledge that God made the pathway to heaven so simple will be the worst torment of all. Yet, they chose rebellion until the end of their lives — unlike the thief on the cross who missed hell by only moments. Accepting the Savior just before giving up the ghost. For the last two thousand years the Lord's mercy has flowed to as many as have accepted the death of His Son for payment of their sins. Knowing this was their only hope.

The Lord is full of mercy. It is His nature. And because of this, the day is coming when His mercy will flow to His church in the most supernatural way imaginable. The day the church is removed from the earth.

CHAPTER ELEVEN

The Resurrection of the Dead and the Rapture

When a loved one is at death's door everything else fades to insignificance. And so it was with Martha and Mary. Their brother Lazarus was very sick. Since he was a personal friend of Jesus they sought to make the Lord aware of his condition knowing He could heal him. So they sent an urgent messenger to Him. Upon receiving the message Jesus waited several days before going to His friend. As a result, when He and the disciples finally arrived Lazarus was already dead.

Knowing Lazarus was a close personal friend of Jesus and that the Lord could have easily healed him, as He had done for so many others, certainly must have puzzled His followers. Why did He delay as His friend lay dying? But unbeknownst to them Jesus was choreographing an event representative of a much greater one yet to come. The miracle of Lazarus being raised from the dead is a brief look into the greatest supernatural event yet to unfold — the future resurrection of the church.

The startling event was spoken of by Jesus and His prophets. John 5 records the Savior describing a scene completely outside the laws of nature where "all who are in the tombs will hear His voice, and will come forth; those who did the good deeds to a resurrection of life, those who committed the evil deeds to a resurrection of judgment." Not only are the dearly departed coming out of tombs en masse, but poor men who could not afford a tomb, "who sleep in the dust of the ground will awake," according to Daniel 12. And the sea containing billions of particles of those who perished within its raging waters they too will arise within this supernatural event according to Revelation 20. Scripture also provides another unassailable statement of truth relating to the resurrection found in 1 Thessalonians 4:15-17.

> [15] For this we say to you by the word of the Lord, that we who are alive and remain until the coming of the Lord will by no means precede those who are asleep. [16] For the Lord Himself will descend from heaven with a shout, with the voice of an archangel, and with the trumpet of God. <u>And the dead in Christ will rise first.</u> [17] <u>Then we who are alive and remain shall be caught up together with them</u> in the clouds to meet the Lord in the air. And thus we shall always be with the Lord.

The mind of man cannot grasp the dead opening their eyes. It is beyond both experience and intellect. Yet, not only will mankind have to process a mass of graves opening to release their dead, but the saved walking the earth will be "caught up" into the air immediately after the dead rise. Both meet somewhere above the earth possibly in full view of a terrified world below. And those fortunate enough to understand the significance of not being caught up will face an added terror. Eternal terror. Perhaps leading to salvation.

In Paul's prophecy, there is a certain order of events. And it is a detail of the utmost importance. He tells us that "the dead in Christ will rise <u>first</u>," and only thereafter "we who are alive and remain shall be caught up together with them in the clouds to meet the Lord in the air." The truth provided by this scripture requires attention because it plays a critical role in determining the season of the resurrection & rapture. Not the day or hour. This is the first precept of truth in the quest for the season.

It is made clear by Paul that you cannot have the rapture without the resurrection of the dead taking place "first!" Perhaps a split second before — but still first. This is not a complicated truth. It is plain and simple. You simply can't have the rapture before the resurrection of the dead. The resurrection of the dead must happen first. But this grand supernatural event of the dead rising out of their graves has another detail associated with it as noted by John the Revelator.

> [4] And I saw thrones, and they sat on them, and judgment was committed to them. Then I saw the souls of those who had been beheaded for their witness to Jesus and for the word of God, who had not worshiped the beast or his image, and had not received his mark on their foreheads or on their hands. And they lived and reigned with Christ for a thousand years. [5] But the rest of the dead did not live again until the thousand years were finished. This is the first resurrection. [6] Blessed and holy is he who has part in the first resurrection. Over such the second death has no power, but they shall be priests of God and of Christ, and shall reign with Him a thousand years. Revelation 20

John tells us how many resurrections of the dead events will take place in the future. And he is talking about general resurrections — en masse — and not specific ones such as what Jesus and Lazarus experienced. John says there are only two mass resurrection events. The "first resurrection" happens before the thousand-year reign of Christ and those participating in it "shall be priests of God and of Christ, and shall reign with Him a thousand years." However, those not participating in the first resurrection face a very different reality. Instead of being resurrected prior to the thousand years reign of Christ, "the rest of the dead did not live again until the thousand years were finished." They are the ones facing the greatest possible terror — eternal condemnation experiencing the "second death" because they rejected Christ.

There are some who try to say that the first resurrection already took place when Christ rose from the dead. But for them, there is this scripture of correction.

> [16] But shun profane and idle babblings, for they will in-crease to more ungodliness. [17] And their message will spread like cancer. Hymenaeus and Philetus are of this sort, [18] who have strayed concerning the truth, saying that the resurrection is already past; and they overthrow the faith of some. 2 Timothy 2

Hymenaeus and Philetus were declared to be speaking "cancer" by making the claim that the resurrection spoken of by the prophets had already taken place. This clearly rules out the possibility that Jesus' resurrection qualified as that first. And the rebuke continues to be directed toward any today who might claim the first resurrection spoken of by John already took place. It has not. To make such a claim remains an act of spreading spiritual cancer. Now there is another warning to be considered when rightly dividing John's words. It is to not play word games with what he says but to accept the details as given.

> [18] For I testify to everyone who hears the words of the prophecy of this book: If anyone adds to these things, God will add to him the plagues that are written in this book; [19] and if anyone takes away from the words of the book of this prophecy, God shall take away his part from the Book of Life, from the holy city, and from the things which are written in this book. Revelation 22:18-19

In the most severe terms, we are advised not to add or remove anything from the verses of Revelation. We are being told that the details of the book are given with a level of precision not to be molested by men. So when John tells us that there is only one resurrection prior to the thousand years, and even labels it the first, he is making it clear there are no resurrections prior to that first one. The Greek word for first is "protos" which means "first in time or place." To say there is another resurrection before John's first substantially alters his words in a clear breach of those warnings.

Some also try to say that the first resurrection spoken of by John is only for the Jews claiming one for Christians takes place before it. But that is to add the word "Jews" to the words of the prophecy in a direct violation of John's warning. It also would force John's first resurrection into becoming the second resurrection by placing one before it. And this too results in a substantial alteration of John's words. Additionally, to claim there will be a "secret" resurrection of the dead not found in scripture runs afoul of Amos 3. Wherein the prophet informs us of the following:

> Surely the Lord GOD does nothing, Unless He reveals His
> secret to His servants the prophets.

He says the Lord will do nothing relative to mankind without telling His prophets which they then tell us. And the resurrection of the dead and rapture are very big somethings. But notice another detail John provides. And it is of the utmost importance concerning the season of the resurrection and rapture.

There are certain martyrs noted as being included in the first resurrection. In other words, they are raised from the dead when the first resurrection takes place. Of course, for that to happen they must first be dead. And this is no flippant observation. It is noteworthy for a reason. The martyrs described in these verses are unique in church history. Since they are those who had been beheaded … and had not worshiped the beast or his image and had not received his mark, those martyrs can only exist during the last half of the seven years. And why is this?

Their refusal to worship the beast is directly related to his sitting in the rebuilt Jewish temple and declaring himself to be God. It is only thereafter that he forces people to worship him or face martyrdom. That seminal prophetic event of defiling the temple does not happen until the mid-point of the seven-year tribulation.

Therefore, since such martyrs cannot exist until the second half of the seven years, and they participate in the first resurrection of the dead, we know the first resurrection of the dead cannot take place until sometime during the second half of the seven years. Otherwise, if it took place before then these specific martyrs could not be included in it. And John is not the only prophet that tells us the resurrection does not happen until the second half of the seven years. The prophet Daniel does so as well. He first establishes the time frame he is speaking about.

> "At that time Michael shall stand up,
> The great prince who stands watch over the sons of your
> people;
> And there shall be a time of trouble,
> Such as never was since there was a nation,
> Even to that time.
> And at that time your people shall be delivered,
> Every one who is found written in the book. Daniel 12

The phrase: "And there shall be a time of trouble, Such as never was since there was a nation, Even to that time," is one that describes the second half of the seven years. We know that because Jesus uses essentially the same phrase in Matthew 24:21. After describing the "abomination of desolation" — the midpoint moment wherein the Antichrist sits in the temple — Jesus goes on to describe the condition of the earth thereafter which is the second half of the seven years:

For then there will be great tribulation, such as has not
been since the beginning of the world until this time, no,
nor ever shall be. Matthew 24:21

Jesus' words are essentially the same as those of Daniel. And since
Jesus makes it clear this time of "great tribulation" takes place after the
"abomination of desolation," then His words describe the second half of
the seven years. Now back to Daniel. After describing the general time
frame as that of the second half Daniel tells us what event takes place then.

> [2] And many of those who sleep in the dust of the earth
> shall awake,
> Some to everlasting life,
> Some to shame and everlasting contempt. Daniel 12:1-2

The description of the dead coming out of the dust of the earth is
of the resurrection of the dead. And since John assures us there is only
one resurrection prior to the thousand years reign of Christ, then the one
Daniel speaks of must also be that same one John mentions. It cannot be
for Jews only as some try to claim. Therefore, two prophets identify the
first and only resurrection of the dead prior to the thousand-year reign of
Christ as not happening until the second half of the seven years.

Since two prophets inform us that the first resurrection does not happen until the second half of the seven years, then a conclusion relative to
the season of the rapture of the church can now be made. And that takes
us back to the words of Paul.

Remember in 1 Thessalonians 4 Paul gave us the Divine order of
supernatural deliverance telling us: "And the dead in Christ will rise
first. [17] Then we who are alive and remain shall be caught up together
with them in the clouds to meet the Lord in the air." He is quite clear that
the rapture cannot take place before the resurrection because "the dead in
Christ will rise first." And since the first resurrection does not take place
until the second half of the seven years, then it is impossible for the rapture

to take place before that time. It is also important to note that although John and Daniel identify the general time frame of the resurrection & rapture, they respect the repeated admonitions in scripture that no man can know "the day or the hour." The words of these prophets are perfectly in line with the statement to know the prophetic season of the church found in 1 Thessalonians 5:1-6.

It is worth repeating that anyone claiming the first resurrection already took place at the time Jesus rose from the dead, taking others out of their graves at that time as well, is spreading spiritual cancer according to 2 Timothy 2:17-18. The rebuke Hymenaeus and Philetus receive in those verses closes the door to claims that Jesus' resurrection represented the mass resurrection of the dead spoken of by His prophets. And remember Paul's words in 1 Thessalonians 4 that the raptured saints will meet the already resurrected ones in the air. To claim the first resurrection already took place at the time of Jesus means the resurrected dead have been waiting in the air for over two thousand years for the raptured saints to arrive!

But Daniel and John are not the only prophets to identify the general time frame of the resurrection & rapture as taking place sometime within the second half of the seven years. Jesus in His Olivet Discourse also comes in agreement with them. He goes as far as to identify where within the Book of Revelation the "blessed hope" takes place leading us right to it.

Jesus' Olivet Discourse

Earlier we looked at the birth pangs beginning of the end times as identified by Jesus in Matthew 24:7-8 — the Olivet Discourse. Whereas then our focus was on the beginning of the end times His discourse stretches all the way to the end as well. And within that expanse of prophetic information, He specifically identifies a global event that must happen before the resurrection & rapture can take place. That event then guides the reader to the Book of Revelation where it is found. Then only seven verses later a description of the resurrection & rapture is found with Jesus taking His "harvest."

But to appreciate His doing this it is first necessary to obtain an understanding of a certain phrase used in the beginning of His Discourse. That phrase represents the last of the three questions asked by His disciples that launches Jesus' response. The question is: When is "the end of the age?" And it is located in Matthew 24:3. A full appreciation of "the end of the age" question is necessary in order to understand the significance of what they are asking Him. Once that phrase is appreciated it is understood that the disciples are directly asking Him when the resurrection & rapture will take place. Then within the Discourse He simply answers their question. So any conversation about the rapture is incomplete without addressing the disciple's final question. To begin the process of appreciating the end of the age question we start with the "wheat and tares" parable in Matthew 13:37-41.

> [37] He answered and said to them: "He who sows the good seed is the Son of Man. [38] The field is the world, the good seeds are the sons of the kingdom, but the tares are the sons of the wicked one. [39] The enemy who sowed them is the devil, the <u>harvest is the end of the age</u>, and the reapers are the angels. "[40] Therefore as the tares are gathered and burned in the fire, so it will be at <u>the end of this age</u>. [41] The Son of Man will send out His angels, and they will gather out of His kingdom all things that offend, and those who practice lawlessness."

Jesus refers to the resurrection & rapture as a harvest to be taken at the end of the age. This appears to be because the removal of believers above and below ground ends the age of the church. Since scripture should be used for defining a phrase based on its usage, then we see what this end of the age phrase means based on Jesus' usage of it. We also gain an appreciation that He views His taking the church as a harvest. This concept of a harvest relates to the notion of the wheat and tares. Only a few verses earlier (29-30) we are told that at the time of the harvest, the wheat will be taken and gathered into His barn. The wheat is, of course, His children. The barn is heaven. But Jesus is not the only prophet that uses this phrase. The prophet Daniel does so as well.

As we saw earlier in Daniel 12 the prophet begins by describing the dead rising out of the "dust of the Earth" in a clear reference to the resurrection of the dead. And this, therefore, is on topic with Jesus' "wheat and tares" explanation which also speaks to the removal of the church from the earth. Then at the end of the chapter Daniel uses a phrase to describe the time of the resurrection. Notice how similar it is to the phrase Jesus used.

> [13] "But you, go your way till the end; for you shall rest, and
> will arise to your inheritance at the end of the days.

In a clear reference to the resurrection of the dead Daniel is told you will "arise to your inheritance" and this happens at "the end of the days." Notice how the phrase is also abbreviated to simply the end. Since this phrase clearly describes Daniel's resurrection then we see why it is almost identical to the phrase "the end of the age" Jesus uses in describing the same event: the resurrection & rapture. The only exception is that one uses the word "days" and the other uses the word "age." And, of course, an age of time is filled with days. So both prophets are effectively using the same phrase to describe the time frame wherein the same event takes place — the resurrection of the dead. If there is any question remaining that they are speaking about the same event that doubt is removed by Martha the sister of Lazarus.

In John 11:24 Martha confronts Jesus for not being there before her brother Lazarus died. In their exchange, she confirms that the resurrection takes place on the "last day."

[24]Martha said to Him, I know that he will rise again in the resurrection at the <u>last day</u>.

Since simple logic demands that "the end of the days" has a "last day," then Jesus and Martha are acknowledging Daniel's description of the time of the resurrection of the dead. And, of course, this must include the rapture since that blessed event cannot happen before the resurrection according to 1 Thessalonian 4. Then there is Jesus Himself directly acknowledging that the resurrection of the dead takes place on the last day in John 6.

> And this is the will of Him who sent Me, that everyone who sees the Son and believes in Him may have everlasting life; and I will raise him up at the <u>last day</u>." John 6:40

Those persons Jesus gives "everlasting life" to He "will raise ... up at the <u>last day</u>." As in resurrecting from the dead. Now consider Paul's usage of the abbreviated term "the end" when speaking directly to the resurrection of the dead at Christ's coming. Paul in 1 Corinthians 15:20-24 tells us:

> [20]But now Christ is risen from the dead, and has become the firstfruits of those who have fallen asleep. [21]For since by man came death, by Man also came the resurrection of the dead. [22]For as in Adam all die, even so in Christ all shall be made alive. [23]But each one in his own order: Christ the firstfruits, afterward those who are Christ's at His coming. [24]Then comes <u>the end</u>, when He delivers the kingdom to God the Father, when He puts an end to all rule and all authority and power.

We are told in these verses that when Christ comes for His own, as in the resurrection & rapture, then comes "the end." Yes, it's the end of the church on earth. This is perfectly in line with Jesus referencing the arrival of "the end of the age" and Daniel's abbreviation "the end" for "the end of the days" in speaking to that same event. Paul is simply using the abbreviated term the end just as Daniel did.

The Olivet Discourse & the End of the Age

Having allowed Jesus, Daniel, and Paul to establish what is meant by the term the end of the age, (and the abbreviated version the end) we return to the Olivet Discourse to consider the implications of its usage there. In Matthew 24:3 we read:

> ³ Now as He sat on the Mount of Olives, the disciples came to Him privately, saying, "Tell us, when will these things be? And what will be the sign of Your coming, and of the end of the age?"

By understanding Jesus, Daniel, and Paul's usage of the term "the end of the age" (and the end) as relating to the time of the resurrection & rapture, we know this question directly relates to the removal of the church from the earth. And this discovery quickly dispels the claim by some that the Olivet Discourse is directed to the Jews only.

As His Discourse progresses we find Jesus referencing back to "the end of the age" question three times using the abbreviated version "the end." The same one used by Daniel and Paul. It is His third reference where Jesus describes a global event that will take place before the end of the age (resurrection & rapture) is reached. Here is the first reference.

> ⁴ And Jesus answered and said to them: "Take heed that no one deceives you. ⁵ For many will come in My name, saying, 'I am the Christ,' and will deceive many. ⁶ And you will hear of wars and rumors of wars. See that you are not troubled; for all these things must come to pass, but the end is not yet.

The second time Jesus references the end of the age question He does so as an assurance to those going through the end times telling them…

¹³ But he who endures to <u>the end</u> shall be saved.

Sure they will be saved. Because according to Jesus at "the end" (of the age) the resurrection & rapture will happen. But His next and final reference to the end of the age question is the one we are looking for. In it, He describes a global event associated with the arrival of the end of the age — the time of the resurrection of the dead and the rapture.

¹⁴ And this gospel of the kingdom will be preached in all the world as a witness to all the nations, and then <u>the end</u> will come.

Nowhere in scripture are we told man accomplishes preaching the gospel to the entire world. Yet, we are told this event must happen before the end of the age (resurrection & rapture) can take place. But there is one place in the Bible where the gospel does get preached to the entire Earth. And it is not man who accomplishes it. But an angel used by God. Then only seven verses later we see Jesus appear on a cloud holding a sickle to reap His harvest. (Think Mt. 13's harvest) This is the resurrection & rapture exactly where Jesus tells us it will be found. First, consider the verses where the gospel finally gets preached to the entire world.

Revelation 14:6-7
⁶ Then I saw another angel flying in the midst of heaven, <u>having the everlasting gospel to preach to those</u> <u>who dwell on the earth—to every nation, tribe, tongue,</u> <u>and people</u>— ⁷ saying with a loud voice, "Fear God and give glory to Him, for the hour of His judgment has come; and worship Him who made heaven and earth, the sea and springs of water."

The gospel just got preached across the Earth in the only place so accomplished in the entire Bible. According to Jesus, we should next see the resurrection & rapture take place. The taking of His "harvest." And seven verses later that is exactly what we see for the only place in the entire Bible.

[14] Then I looked, and behold, a white cloud, and on the cloud sat One like the Son of Man, having on His head a golden crown, and in His hand a sharp sickle. [15] And another angel came out of the temple, crying with a loud voice to Him who sat on the cloud, "Thrust in Your sickle and reap, for the time has come for You to reap, for the harvest of the earth is ripe." [16] So He who sat on the cloud thrust in His sickle on the earth, and the earth was reaped. Revelation 14:14-16

Remember in the explanation of the "wheat and tares" parable Jesus compared His taking the church to that of a harvest, and He defined it as happening at the end of the age. And then in answering the disciple's questions in His Olivet Discourse, He responded that the end of the age won't happen until the gospel is preached to the entire world. Then after seeing it preached to the entire world in Revelation, seven verses later we see Jesus appear on a cloud to take His church in what is described as a harvest. In a moment we'll see how scripture does not allow this event to be the second coming and Armageddon. But first consider how other rapture scriptures, particularly that of 1 Corinthians 15:51-52 and 1 Thessalonians 4:17, were just fulfilled. First, consider 1 Corinthians 15:51-52:

> [51] Behold, I tell you a mystery: We shall not all sleep, but we
> shall all be changed— [52] in a moment, in the twinkling of an
> eye, at the last trumpet. For the trumpet will sound, and the
> dead will be raised incorruptible, and we shall be changed.

And now 1 Thessalonians 4:17:

> [17] Then we who are alive and remain shall be caught up
> together with them in the clouds to meet the Lord in the
> air. And thus we shall always be with the Lord.

Note the following details: the resurrection & rapture is called a "mystery," it is at the "last trumpet," and Jesus is in the "clouds" when it happens and not standing on the earth. Now consider their fulfillment starting with Revelation 10:7

> [7] but in the days of the sounding of the <u>seventh angel,</u>
> when he is about to sound, the <u>mystery of God</u> would
> be finished, as He declared to His servants the prophets.

We are told the "mystery of God" will be finished at the sounding of the trumpet of the seventh angel. That angel sounds in Revelation 12 and that trumpet is the last trumpet in the Book of Revelation. So Jesus' coming for His church in Revelation 14 is after the "last trumpet" sounds and this trumpet, we are specifically told, resolves "the mystery of God … declared to His prophets." In further fulfillment, Jesus is sitting on a cloud. And in fulfillment of Matthew 13 He is taking His harvest which is equated therein to the church. Now consider why this event cannot be Jesus' second coming which happens at the end of the seven-year tribulation.

Few would dispute that Revelation 19 has the second coming described within it. In that description we find Jesus:

- On a white horse
- He has a sword
- He is going to war.

However, in Revelation 14 Jesus is:

- Sitting on a cloud... not riding a white horse
- Holding a sickle... not a sword
- Taking His harvest... not going to war

Obviously, these are two separate events involving Jesus. And since based on its description Revelation 14:14-16 can't be the second coming,

THE END OF THE AGE

then it has to be the resurrection & rapture exactly where Jesus said it would be. Now to address a final claim relating to Jesus' appearance here. Some persons engage in blending verses 14-16 wherein Jesus takes His harvest (church), with the following bloody verses of 17-20 in which grapes of wrath are taken. But there is a problem in so doing. Such an action violates a clear and observable structure within Revelation 14 designed to keep events separate. This was covered earlier as well.

You will notice there are six descriptions of events and admonitions in chapter 14 kept separate by the use of announcing angels. These five announcing angels are strategically placed between each of the six events to prevent their being blended together. So blending together the last two events to make verses 14-16 & 17-20 appear to be a single event that includes much blood and violence violates this structure. All it takes is a quick peruse of the chapter to confirm this.

1ˢᵗ **Event Verses 1-5:** Descriptions of the 144,000

Announcing Angel # 1 in Verse 6

2ⁿᵈ **Event Verses 6-7:** Gospel preached across the earth

Announcing Angel # 2 in Verse 8

3ʳᵈ **Event Verse 8:** Mystery Babylon

Announcing Angel # 3 in Verse 9

4ᵗʰ **Event Verses 9-13:** Admonitions against giving in to the beast

Announcing Angel # 4 in Verse 15

5ᵗʰ **Event Verses 14-16:** Jesus taking the harvest of His church

Announcing Angel # 5 in Verse 17

6ᵗʰ **Event Verses 17-20:** Very likely the Battle of Armageddon

As is obvious the structure in Revelation 14 is designed to keep separate the six events described therein. And this clearly distinguishes Jesus' harvesting of His church in verses 14-16 from the next event in verses

17-20, announced by yet another angel in verse 17, which is the Battle of
Armageddon due to the "grapes of wrath" reference within it. (Grapes of
wrath are also used in Revelation 19 and Joel 3:12-13 — as well as the
second Valley of Jehoshaphat judgment — to describe Armageddon.)

Jesus appearing in verse 14 to take His harvest (church) is why earlier in the chapter we are told "firstfruits" are taken. Consider that the
"hundred forty and four thousand" servants of God are "redeemed from
among men, being the firstfruits unto God and to the Lamb." And
there is no indication they were killed. They are apparently the last of
the firstfruits before the actual harvest (Remember MT 13 used harvest
to indicate the Resurrection & Rapture) is taken only a few verses later.
The resurrection of Jesus is also considered that of firstfruits. Firstfruits
are always taken before the harvest. And, of course, Revelation 14 covers major events that will take place during the second half of the seven
years. So this taking of His harvest happens sometime therein — the
second half — the same season both John the Revelator and Daniel
the prophet indicates the resurrection of the dead takes place. And you
can't have the rapture before the resurrection of the dead according to
1 Thessalonians 4. Now consider the significance of Jesus' words at the
start of His Discourse in Matthew 24 and how here, too, He rules out an
earlier resurrection & rapture.

The End is Not Yet

We just looked at how Jesus takes the disciple's last question — when is the
end of the age — and brings us to its literal fulfillment in Revelation 14.
He told us about the seminal event that must happen first — preaching
the gospel to the entire world. And we found that fulfilled in Revelation
14. Then a few verses later we saw Jesus on a cloud taking His harvest.
Now we will look at how Jesus rules out an early resurrection & rapture
at the start of His Discourse.

The significance of the term "the end of the age" was defined for us by Jesus, Daniel, and Paul as the season of the resurrection & rapture. Keeping that in mind we then see in His Discourse Jesus starts by first warning against falling victim to deception.

> ⁴And Jesus answered and said unto them, Take heed that
> no man deceive you. ⁵For many shall come in my name,
> saying, I am Christ; and shall deceive many.

Then He describes a time of "wars and rumors of wars." But notice how He specifically identifies this time frame as not yet "the end."

> ⁶And ye shall hear of wars and rumours of wars: see that
> ye be not troubled: for all these things must come to pass,
> but <u>the end is not yet</u>.

After describing that time He specifically says "but <u>the end</u> is not yet." And this is His first response to their "end of the age" question. He uses the same abbreviated version of the end of the age phrase that both Daniel and Paul used going out of His way to let us know the end of the age will not happen during this time of "wars and rumors of wars." Why is that so important? Because the next verse can be isolated as the start of the day of the Lord. This was shown in chapter one Warning Signs. This is because Jesus describes it's events as birth pangs. Remember the sudden beginning of the day of the Lord is described as birth pangs in 1 Thessalonians 5:1-3. And we know the Holy Spirit is consistent. Yet, we are specifically told just before it starts that "the end (of the age) is not yet." Here are the next verses that launch the day of the Lord.

> ⁷For nation shall rise against nation, and kingdom against
> kingdom: and there shall be famines, and pestilences, and
> earthquakes, in divers places. ⁸All these are <u>the beginning</u>
> <u>of sorrows.</u>

The word used for the "beginning of sorrows" is the Greek verb "odin" — birth pangs. The exact same word used in 1 Thessalonians 5:1-3 in describing birth pangs as the start of the day of the Lord. It's the start of the end times. In doing this Jesus rules out an early resurrection & rapture by telling us the end of the age does not happen before the day of the Lord begins. But Jesus has even more to say in His Discourse on the topic.

After a Time of Tribulation

The Lord tells us in Matthew 24:29 "Immediately after the tribulation of those days that the Son of Man (will be) coming on the clouds ... And He will send His angels with a great sound of a trumpet, and they will gather together His elect from the four winds, from one end of heaven to the other." It is clear that the Son of Man comes on the clouds to take His elect after a period of tribulation. And within the Discourse this declaration comes only after Jesus describes the event that marks the end of the age which we looked at wherein the preaching of the gospel to the entire earth led us directly to Revelation 14. Some try to say this passage is referring to the second coming claiming the gathering of the elect from the four winds, from one end of Heaven to the other refers to gathering the elect within heaven proper — God's abode. But here is why that is a false claim.

The "four winds, from one end of heaven to the other" phrase we know refers to events across the Earth itself and not heaven proper based on prior usage. The scriptures showing this are Daniel 8:8-9, Jeremiah 49:35-37, and Nehemiah 1:8-9. Additionally, a particular detail is provided of what happens when those angels take the elect. As the description of this event continues we are told in verse "⁴⁰Then two men will be in the field: one will be taken and the other left. ⁴¹ Two women will be grinding at the mill: one will be taken and the other left." What a great description of the rapture... Immediately after the tribulation of those days.

It must be that by telling us "after the tribulation of those days" Jesus is referring to after a segment of tribulation that unfolds during the second half and not after the second half. This is based on Daniel 12. Therein Daniel indicates the resurrection & rapture take place sometime within the second half. Remember his words.

After describing "a time of trouble, Such as never was since there was a nation, Even to that time," Daniel tells us "at that time" the resurrection will take place. That means during the second half and not after. Once the end times are over then the second half has ended. So if the resurrection of the dead took place after the last half — post-tribulation — then his words at that time would be inaccurate. But Daniel is clear the second half of the seven years will still be ongoing when the dead rise. So the resurrection & rapture does not happen post-tribulation, but sometime during the last half of the seven years after a time of tribulation. This is the season and not "the day or hour." But there is more.

There is also Paul speaking to the Thessalonians wherein he too places "the coming of our Lord Jesus Christ and by our gathering together unto him" — the resurrection & rapture — as not happening until the second half of the seven years.

Paul and the Day of Christ

In 2 Thessalonians 2:1-6 KJV Paul provides an excellent description of the resurrection & rapture. And he too indicates the general time frame wherein it takes place. Not the day or the hour. He tells us it will not happen until after the Antichrist sits in the temple and there is a "falling away" from the faith. And, of course, the Antichrist sits in the rebuilt Jewish temple at the midpoint of the seven-year tribulation. Consider the verses:

> ¹Now we beseech you, brethren, by the coming of our Lord
> Jesus Christ, and by our gathering together unto him,
> ² That ye be not soon shaken in mind, or be troubled,
> neither by spirit, nor by word, nor by letter as from us, as
> that the day of Christ is at hand.

³ Let no man deceive you by any means: for that day shall not come, except there come <u>a falling away first, and that man of sin be revealed,</u> the son of perdition;

⁴ Who opposeth and exalteth himself above all that is called God, or that is worshipped; so that <u>he as God sitteth in the temple of God, shewing himself that he is God.</u>

⁵<u>Remember ye not, that, when I was yet with you, I told you these things?</u>

⁶ And now ye know what withholdeth that he might be revealed in his time.

⁷ For the mystery of iniquity doth already work: only he who now letteth will let, until he be taken out of the way.

(King James Version)

Paul joins Jesus, John, and Daniel in placing the resurrection & rapture as happening sometime within the 2ⁿᵈ half of the seven-year tribulation — after the Antichrist "sitteth in the temple of God" and after a period of tribulation. In these verses Paul is specific and clear he is referring to the "day of Christ ... the coming of our Lord Jesus Christ and our gathering together to Him," and not the day of the Lord as some try to say. The Greek word used in the verse is "Christos." And any question as to if the day of Christ refers to the second coming — instead of the resurrection & rapture — is quickly dispelled by a reading of Philippians 1. That chapter contains two references to the day of Christ, or a derivative of it, telling us that believers are on the earth still being perfected until the day of Christ. We know this perfecting ends at the rapture and not the second coming. And in 2 Thessalonians 2:3 Paul then ruggedly declares that anyone teaching another sequence of events is engaged in deception.

Also, notice Paul's admonition in verse 2 against those claiming "the day of Christ" could be "at hand" as though it could happen at any moment. This is a clear swipe against those embracing the so-called "Imminence doctrine" currently popular within certain circles. Forgetting that scripture repeatedly tells us it is the day or the hour we cannot know and not the season. The word used for at hand is the Greek verb "enistemi" meaning "impend, threaten, close at hand, or present" and the KJV best relays this. The verses then go on to tell about the removal of the Holy Spirit as a restraint on identifying Antichrist. But nowhere do these verses tell us the Holy Spirit is removed from the Earth as some also try to say.

Paul informs us that this removal of restraint in identifying the Antichrist is associated with the mid-point when the Beast sits in the temple. This means the restraint is removed for the 2nd half of the seven-year tribulation. And his words dovetail nicely with Daniel 12:4 & 9 describing the sealing of information until "the time of the end." And, of course, the time of the end is also the 2nd half of the seven year tribulation as we have repeatedly seen. Yet, Daniel 12:10 says "the wise shall understand" and Paul joins him entreating that this knowledge is available in spite of a sealing or restraint on it. So why do both 2 Thessalonians 2 and Daniel 12 indicate knowledge is restrained or sealed until the 2nd half for the unwise only? When considering the context of these scriptures the most logical answer seems to be that it takes Antichrist sitting in the temple at the mid-point to open the eyes of those embracing a false teaching relating to the season of "the day of Christ" — the time of the resurrection & rapture. Apparently, Antichrist sitting in the temple shocks them out of their error.

> **Author's Note:** Some challenge that 2 Thessalonians 2:2 reads "the day of Christ" claiming it actually reads "the day of the Lord." This is due to differences in old manuscripts. And reading it "the day of the Lord" would eliminate its usefulness to the resurrection & rapture topic. This challenge is addressed in Addendum 2 in the back of the book. Therein it is explained that if it reads "the day of the Lord," instead of "the day of Christ," then two irreconcilable conflicts arise with Paul's previous words in 1 Thessalonians 5.

If that "falling away" of believers in 2 Thessalonians 2 is the result of them seeing the Antichrist sitting in the temple after having been taught they would be raptured before that blasphemy happens, then it may represent a devastating reverse ministry calculated to the eternal rewards ledger of those teaching something other than what the prophets are telling us.

Seeing that the day of Christ refers to the time of the resurrection & rapture and that this time is called the end of the age, or the abbreviated version of simply the end according to Jesus, Daniel, and Paul, consider how Paul in 1 Corinthians 1:7-8 connects the day of Christ with the end.

>...eagerly waiting for the revelation of our Lord Jesus Christ, [8] who will also confirm you to <u>the end</u>, that you may be blameless in <u>the day of our Lord Jesus Christ.</u>

We are told how Jesus confirms us until the end (of the age) keeping His own blameless until His day for taking His church arrives. And this day is the day of our Lord Jesus Christ, the longer variation of the term the day of Christ.

The Times of the Gentiles

There are many who believe that when the church is removed from the world, through the resurrection & rapture "the times of the Gentiles" comes to an abrupt end. This topic too is addressed by the prophets. In Luke's account of the Olivet Discourse, we are told the following concerning the times of the Gentiles.

[24] And they shall fall by the edge of the sword, and shall be led away captive into all nations: and Jerusalem shall be <u>trodden</u> down of the Gentiles, until the <u>times of the Gentiles be fulfilled</u>. Luke 21:24

We are told in the clearest terms possible that as long as the City of Jerusalem is being "trodden down" by Gentiles, the times of the Gentiles will continue. And the flip side of that coin would indicate that when the troddening down stops so too does the times of the Gentiles. The word used for "trodden" is the Greek verb "pateo." Now consider John's words in Revelation 11:1-2 relating to the Gentiles treading underfoot the city of Jerusalem during the end times. He is specific and clear.

> [1]And there was given me a reed like unto a rod: and the angel stood, saying, Rise, and measure the temple of God, and the altar, and them that worship therein. [2]But the court which is without the temple leave out, and measure it not; for it is given unto the Gentiles: and the holy city shall they **tread** under foot forty and two months.

John tells us that the Gentiles will "tread (trodden) under foot ... the holy city" (Jerusalem) for the first 42 months of the seven years. But no longer. Just the first half of the seven years. That means that the times of the Gentiles cannot come to an end until after the first half. The word used for tread is "pateo" the same Greek verb used in Luke 21. This is perfectly in line with Jesus, Daniel, John, and Paul telling us that the resurrection of the dead and the rapture do not happen until the second half of the seven years. (Addendum 3 in the back of the book covers some pre-trib. counter-points.)

According to the prophets, it is clear that the resurrection of the dead and the rapture do not take place until sometime within the second half of the seven years. This makes sense. The story of the Bible and creation itself is about the glory and majesty of the Lord. And He is most glorified when His children do "not love their lives to the death" for His sake. The benefits His children receive for doing so are both great and eternal. And the greatest opportunity for achieving both the glorification of the Lord, and eternal benefits for His children, is during the end times. To think the Lord would short-circuit the season for both to unfold on the grandest scale ever is unthinkable. Although we cannot know the day or the hour we do know the season because...

> Surely the Lord God does nothing, unless He reveals His secret to His servants the prophets. Amos 3:7

CHAPTER TWELVE

About Those End Time
Birth Pangs

O ver the last century, the Christian church has witnessed Western culture experience a dramatic decline in morals and ethics. Whereas across the ages sin was usually a thing of shame, in the current day the stigma is gone. According to 2 Timothy 3, such a state of degradation has been expected. And just as this unhappy development has quickened mankind has experienced advances in technology that have accelerated at a dizzying pace. Yet, the latter needs the former as a governor. The result has been an ill-conceived mixture of great destructive power in the hands of those least suited morally and ethically to handle it. Producing the most explosive and dangerous cocktail the world has ever seen. And this development has not gone unnoticed within church circles. As a result, there are teachers and students of Bible prophecy that have been nudged by this development into making claims that are not yet supported by the facts. One such claim relates to end time birth pangs having already begun.. Confusing general birth pangs — which have been accelerating — with those that launch the day of the Lord.

When end time birth pangs are discussed what is typically cited is a particular war or earthquake that suddenly strikes. When this happens much is made out of it citing Jesus's words of wars and earthquakes in Matthew 24. Although He speaks about such a time of "wars and rumors of wars," that time does not represent birth pangs. But events prior to them. Actual birth pangs start with the "sudden destruction" of a great war pitting "nation against nation, and kingdom against kingdom." For all practical purposes, it is World War III. The sudden launch of birth pangs will also include "great (Greek "megas") earthquakes" across the entire earth.

John the Revelator identifies Jesus' birth pangs war as the rider of the "red horse" of the apocalypse. Paul in 1 Thessalonians 5 notes the destruction of this great war comes as "sudden destruction" indicating the nations are not in general conflict before it begins. Jesus also makes it clear the nations will not be in a state of general warfare before it begins because they must "rise" to war. The birth pangs beginning of the end times don't just creep up on the world. They come suddenly "like a thief in the night" according to Paul.

The perspective that the world is experiencing end time birth pangs is for two reasons. The first is that the world is seeing a multitude of end time signs. The second is a wrong definition of what end time birth pangs are. This centers on the belief that end time birth pangs are "the increasing intensity of events." But the true definition based on actual usage is "the sudden beginning of God's wrath." As an array of scripture indicates end time birth pangs begin suddenly and with great fury. They may increase in intensity thereafter, but their start is sudden and with great force. As a result, before birth pangs begin the armies of the world should NOT be in a state of general warfare. This relative state of peace between nations sets the stage for them to "rise" into "sudden destruction" just as Jesus and Paul indicated they would at its start. Yes, there will still be wars happening. There always have been. But the launch of end time birth pangs is that of a world war suddenly starting. Has that happened as of 2024? But relating to general warfare consider the following scholarly academic report on warfare to establish a factual perspective.

> "The period since 1945 arguably represents the longest
> period of great power peace since the birth of the modern
> world system in 1495."[1]

In a series of academic studies focusing on the phenomenon of war, one thing is clear — as of 2024 warfare between nations has been trending down since the end of World War II. This is true in spite of there being some notable wars taking place. Because there always are some wars taking place. In fact, one such study speculates that the current relative lack of warfare between nation-states might be at its lowest point since the year 1495! Those studies have led to articles with titles like, "Think Again: War…World Peace Could be Closer than you Think[2]" in the prestigious *Foreign Policy* magazine, and "War Really is Going Out of Style"[3] published in *The New York Times*. However, this new condition among the nations does not mean warfare between nations has completely stopped. And a case in point is the current war between Russia and Ukraine. But in spite of that and other wars the fact is that warfare is still at an extremely low point. In fact, warfare between nations is actually trending dramatically downward as an array of statistics show.

Warfare between the Nations

In searching for the true facts relating to nation-to-nation warfare consider the following quotes taken from a paper published in International Studies Quarterly (2003) titled: *Inter-State, Intra-State, and Extra-State Wars: A Comprehensive Look at Their Distribution over Time, 1816-1997.* The paper is a compilation of not less than 53 studies on warfare produced by a multitude of academic scholars across the world. Read how clear they are about the subject of warfare between nations.

[1]"the period since 1945 arguably represents the longest period of great power peace since the birth of the modern world system in 1495." Pp 52

"world more peaceful than at any time in the past century." Pp 52

"Many scholars have noted a decreasing propensity for states to go to war. For instance, Levy detected a downward trend in great power wars (wars in which at least one major sovereign state fought on each of the two sides) over the period

1495–1975." Pp 51

"Discussions of the decline in warfare (between nations) have become more pronounced when dealing with the post–World War II era." Pp 51

Here are the references to those quotes:

[1]**Study Link:** http://deepblue.lib.umich.edu/bitstream/handle/2027.42/71639/1468-2478.4701003.pdf?sequence=1&isAllowed=y
[2]Foreignpolicy.com/2011/08/15/think-again-war/
[3]http://www.nytimes.com/2011/12/18/opinion/sunday/war-really-is-going-out-of-style.html?_r=0
[4]http://www.politifact.com/punditfact/statements/2014/jul/21/stu-burguiere/fewer-wars-fewer-people-dying-wars-now-quite-some/

As a result of this strange lack of warfare between nations, there has been a dramatic decline in "Battle Deaths" since the end of World War II as the following chart from *Our World in Data* shows.

Death rate in state-based conflicts, World

Deaths of combatants and civilians due to fighting, per 100,000 people. Included are interstate¹, intrastate², and extrasystemic³ conflicts that were ongoing that year.

Our World in Data

- Extrasystemic
- Intrastate
- Interstate

Data source: Uppsala Conflict Data Program (2023); Peace Research Institute Oslo (2017); Population based on various sources (2023)
OurWorldInData.org/war-and-peace | CC BY

1. **Interstate conflict (UCDP and PRIO):** A conflict between states that causes at least 25 deaths during a year. This includes combatant and civilian deaths due to fighting, but excludes deaths due to disease and starvation resulting from the conflict.

2. **Intrastate conflict (UCDP and PRIO):** A conflict between a state and a non-state armed group inside the state's territory that causes at least 25 deaths during a year. This includes combatant and civilian deaths due to fighting, but excludes deaths due to disease and starvation resulting from the conflict. If a foreign state is involved, it is called "internationalized", and "non-internationalized" otherwise.

3. **Extrasystemic conflict (UCDP and PRIO):** A conflict between a state and a non-state armed group outside the state's territory that causes at least 25 deaths during a year. This includes combatant and civilian deaths due to fighting, but excludes deaths due to disease and starvation resulting from the conflict.

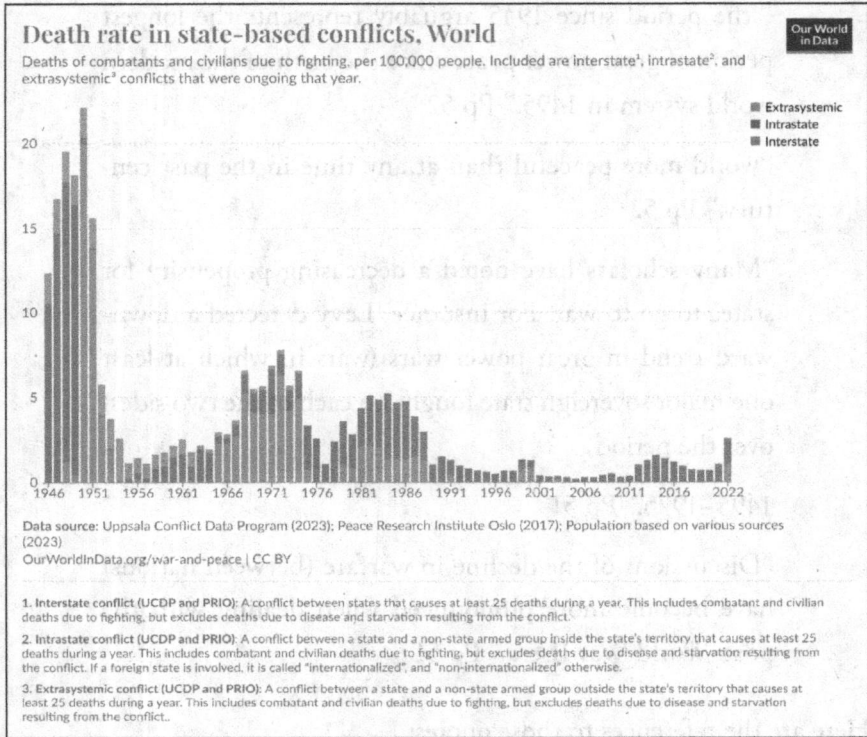

It is obvious that Jesus' admonition of "nation shall rise against nation" at the launch of birth pangs has not yet happened. In line with that neither has Paul's "sudden destruction" or, for that matter, nor has John's "red horse" begun galloping. In fact, the world is more peaceful relative to warfare between nations than at any time since the year 1495. This is perfectly in line with the condition that should exist prior to the sudden launch of birth pangs. The current low level of nation-to-nation warfare lines up with the nations needing to "rise" to war when birth pangs begin. And as this condition exists Israel is fulfilling the pre-birth pangs wars of Matthew 24:6. This is also why those "wars and rumors of wars" should apply to Israel and not the nations.

The likely reason for this dramatic reduction in major warfare is the prevalence of nuclear weapons. Their existence not only raises the stakes of conflict to an unacceptable point causing warfare to dramatically decline, but also sets the stage for the massive sudden destruction indicated in the scriptures at its beginning.

Now consider earthquake activity across the world today compared to ones expected during prophetic birth pangs. This is according to Luke 21. Remember in Luke's version of Jesus' Olivet Discourse he gives us a qualifier concerning these earthquakes. He tells us the birth pangs of the end times will launch with "great" earthquakes all over the earth. But that too has not yet begun.

Great Earthquakes in Divers Places

Ask anyone who follows Bible prophecy if recent earthquake activity matches what the Scriptures tell us to look for when end time birth pangs begin. And 9 out of 10 will likely offer an emphatic YES! But like so many traditions of men that circulate as truth reality is quite different. First, consider again what the Scriptures have to say concerning the earthquakes that will accompany the start of the end times beginning with Matthew 24:6-8.

> [6] And ye shall hear of wars and rumours of wars: see that ye be not troubled: for all these things must come to pass, but the end is not yet.
>
> [7] For nation shall rise against nation, and kingdom against kingdom: and there shall be famines, and pestilences, and earthquakes, in divers places.
>
> [8] All these are the beginning of sorrows.

As we saw earlier Matthew tells us the signs that accompany the start of the end times in verse 7 and we are told earthquakes will be taking place "in divers places." The word used for divers is the Greek preposition "kata" which means "though out." But since earthquakes have been taking place "though out" the world for thousands of years, this Scripture alone doesn't really help to determine if birth pangs have begun. All we know from it is that there will be earthquakes all over the earth. However, Luke 21:9-11 covers the same end time beginning events as Matthew 24:6-8 but adds a detail to the type of earthquakes they will be. And this allows us to become much more precise in what to look for.

> ⁹ But when ye shall hear of wars and commotions, be not terrified: for these things must first come to pass; but the end is not by and by.
>
> ¹⁰ Then said he unto them, Nation shall rise against nation, and kingdom against kingdom:
>
> ¹¹ And **great** earthquakes shall be in divers places, and famines, and pestilences; and fearful sights and great signs shall there be from heaven.

Here we are provided a significant qualifier that eliminates the overwhelming majority of earthquakes that take place each year. We are told the earthquakes that will be all over the earth at the launch of the end times will be "great" ones. So to determine exactly what is meant by the term "great" let's look now at how it is used elsewhere in Luke.

The term "great" is used 38 times in the Book of Luke to describe something or someone that is extraordinary. For example, in Luke 1:15 John the Baptist is referred to as great. In fact, he was considered so great that Jesus indicates he was the greatest among men. And that is significant greatness. In Luke 1:32 Jesus is referred to as great as well as the multitudes that followed Jesus in Luke 5:15. The word used for great is the Greek adjective "megas" which produces our English word "mega" for something that is incredibly large or significant. The key understanding here is that this term is used to impart an exceptional nature to that which it is being applied. So the earthquakes associated with the birth pangs launch of the day of the Lord will be extraordinarily significant ones. They will be "mega" earthquakes. Now consider what the United

States Geological Survey (U.S.G.S.) says about "mega" earthquakes over the last 100 years.

In an article published on April 17, 2016, after a series of earthquakes rocked Japan and Ecuador, the U.S.G.S. indicated there have been <u>no</u> "mega" earthquakes since seismic activity has been measured over the last 100 years. And this statement was issued after earthquakes of 7.3 and 7.8 had just been recorded. On the U.S.G.S. website, the following is a good summation of their answer to the question if "mega" earthquakes are even possible:

> "Theoretically yes, but realistically the answer is probably no… Scientists, however, can't rule out a "mega" quake because they've only been measuring earthquakes for 100 years."

But for the sake of those insisting on their own definition of what constitutes great (megas) earthquakes, consider the following graph using 8.0 and higher earthquake activity by decade between the years 1900 and 2024.

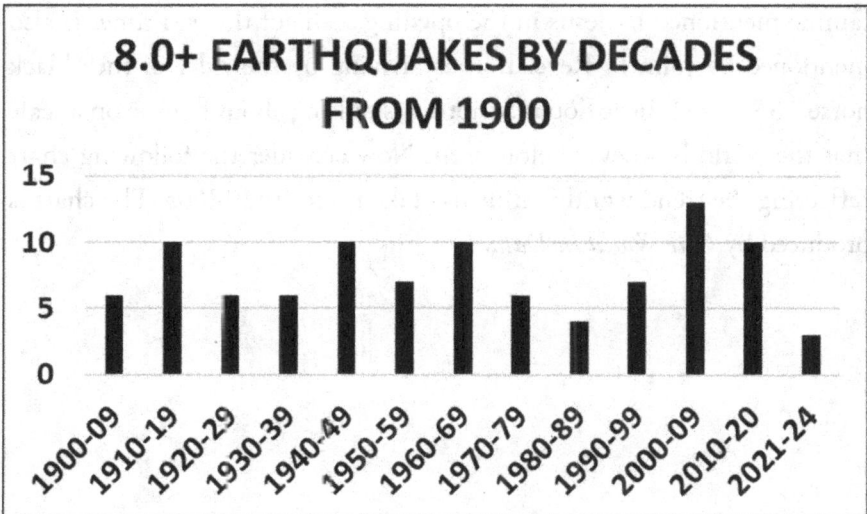

8.0+ EARTHQUAKES BY DECADES FROM 1900

To verify these results simply go to the following link and you can plug in the criteria yourself. http://earthquake.usgs.gov/earthquakes/search/

It is clear from those graphs that significant earthquakes have not been increasing across the earth since the year 1900. There is something else to consider. In the first four decades of the last century, there were not as many seismometers placed across the world. As a result, some number of large earthquakes went unrecorded. So those numbers are understated which further emphasizes the lack of an increase in "great" earthquakes in the present day. Remember the scriptural requirement for earthquake activity that accompanies the start of end time birth pangs is great (mega) earthquakes all over the surface of the earth. Since this is what the scriptures call for, and the above graphs are an accurate reflection of the lack of mega or great earthquakes across the earth, it is easy to reach a solid conclusion: No... the earthquakes that accompany birth pangs have not yet started.

Famines

As we know from Jesus' words in the Olivet Discourse when prophetic birth pangs begin it will also include notable famine. Additionally, the famine mentioned by Jesus in the opening scene of the end times is also mentioned by John in Revelation as arriving by the rider of the "black horse." So there is little doubt Scripture is talking about famine on a scale that the world has never before seen. Now consider the following chart reflecting the trend world famine has taken since the 1860s. The chart is produced by *Our World in Data*.

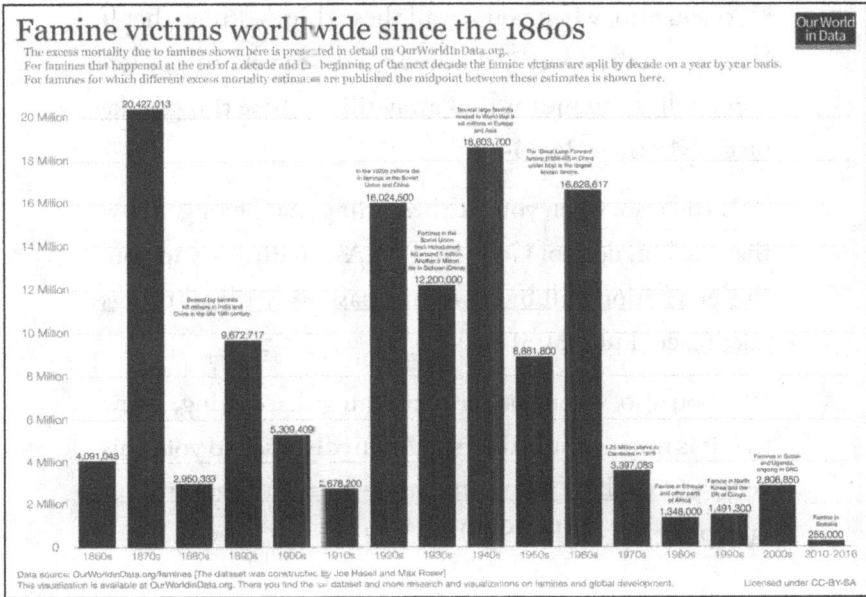

Famine victims worldwide since the 1860s

The excess mortality due to famines shown here is presented in detail on OurWorldInData.org.
For famines that happened at the end of a decade and the beginning of the next decade the famine victims are split by decade on a year by year basis.
For famines for which different excess mortality estimates are published the midpoint between these estimates is shown here.

As the chart clearly shows world famine has declined dramatically over the last 150 years. Disproving any claims that the famines associated with end time birth pangs have begun.

So based on accurate statistics the wars, earthquakes, and famines associated with end time birth pangs have not yet begun. But due to the severity of each described in Scripture when they do suddenly begin the world will know it without any doubt.

Stretching Out the Time Frame

Some try to find events across a length of time to meet the requirements of end time birth pangs. One method they use is to connect major historical events that span many decades or even centuries. However, there is a scriptural problem with that approach. In all three recordings of Jesus' Olivet Discourse, we are given a time limitation on their completion. Here is that admonition in all three recordings of the Discourse:

[33] So you also, when you see all these things, know that it is near—at the doors! [34] Assuredly, I say to you, <u>this generation will by no means pass away till all these things take place</u>. Matthew 24:33-34

[31] So you also, when you see these things happening, know that the kingdom of God is near. [32] Assuredly, I say to you, <u>this generation will by no means pass away till all things take place</u>. Luke 21:31-32

[29] So you also, when you see these things happening, know that it is near—at the doors! [30] Assuredly, I say to you, <u>this generation will by no means pass away till all these things take place</u>. Mark 13:29-30

The day of the Lord which is the end times will be witnessed by a single generation. It will not stretch out over centuries or even decades according to Jesus. As we know the day of the Lord encompasses both birth pangs as well as the seven years. It is a confined time frame. This blocks attempts by some to create the appearance that the end times have begun by simply expanding the time frame considered. Those disposed to do this are attempting to fit events. But Jesus' words appear to be an additional Divine guardrail erected to keep people on the correct track. This guardrail prevents the inclusion of the World Wars of the twentieth century as end time events.

Summation

It is clear that prophetic birth pangs are not defined as "the increasing intensity of events, but through scriptural usage, they are "the sudden beginning of God's wrath." As such it is also clear according to geopolitical and geological facts that they have not yet begun as of the year 2024.

CHAPTER THIRTEEN

The World Condition Prior to End Time Birth Pangs

The "sudden destruction" of the end times starts with birth pangs. These are very specific birth pangs and not to be confused with general birth pangs described in Romans 8. Paul writing in 1 Thessalonians 5 tells us… "For when they say, "Peace and safety!" then sudden destruction comes upon them, as labor pains upon a pregnant woman. And they shall not escape." And with each passing day, that unparalleled time of destruction moves one day closer. Although "that day or hour no man knows," we are equally assured that we will know the season if we are sober.

> ⁴ But you, brethren, are not in darkness, so that this Day should overtake you as a thief. ⁵ You are all sons of light and sons of the day. We are not of the night nor of darkness. ⁶ Therefore let us not sleep, as others do, but let us watch and be sober. 1 Thessalonians 5:4-6

And His prophet Amos tells us…

[7]Surely the Lord GOD does nothing,
Unless He reveals His secret to His servants the prophets.
Amos 3

Indeed, He has revealed to His prophets the specific signs that birth pangs are about to start. And those signs are clear. First, there is a notable war associated with some kind of "wonders in the heavens." This war likely involves Israel as well as the possible use of tactical nuclear weapons. In response to this war, there is then a Peace agreement forced upon the Jewish state by "all nations" removing a portion of her land. The United Nations. And, finally, the heavenly sign of the sun darkening and the moon to blood. Which at the time they unfold should be recognizable to those who are sober. Once these specific signs start they should unfold quickly. But there are other signs as well. They are ones that are general in nature being a condition of the culture and could last a long time before those specific signs begin unfolding.

One general condition has to do with the character of men. Mankind's character will plunge into the abyss of a moral sewer. One unfortunate description of this condition is found in 2 Timothy 3. We are told men will become...

> ...boasters, proud, blasphemers, disobedient to parents,
> unthankful, unholy, [3] unloving, unforgiving, slanderers,
> without self-control, brutal, despisers of good, [4] traitors,
> headstrong, haughty, lovers of pleasure rather than lovers
> of God, [5] having a form of godliness but denying its power.
> 2 Timothy 3

All of the deplorable worldly characteristics of men will become amplified. Even boasted about. An intensity of moral decay covering the world like a cloak of shame. This sad condition will produce distorted cultural offspring such as massive crime, continuous scandals, acceptance of sexual sin, deception without restraint, adultery and divorce as a practice, and even altering the definition of marriage to suit sinful lusts. Jude broadens the picture...

> ¹⁶ These are grumblers, complainers, walking according to their own lusts; and they mouth great swelling words, flattering people to gain advantage. ¹⁷ But you, beloved, remember the words which were spoken before by the apostles of our Lord Jesus Christ: ¹⁸ how they told you that there would be mockers in the last time who would walk according to their own ungodly lusts. ¹⁹ These are sensual persons, who cause divisions, not having the Spirit. Jude 1:16-19

"Not having the Spirit" the unsaved are a plague bacillus on planet Earth. Not only do they practice opposition to God, but now they mock those who follow Him. The stench of moral decay will reach its fullness filling the nostrils of righteous men. And some churches at that time will not only exist in the world which is a necessity, but will struggle not to be a part of it. Pastors tickling the ears of the sheep causing them to sleep when they should be sober and awake. It will be a time of deception within the church. That story is told by Jesus in His Olivet Discourse.

> And Jesus answered and said to them: "Take heed that no one deceives you. ⁵ For many will come in My name, saying, 'I am the Christ,' and will deceive many. Matthew 24:4

Those deceiving come in His name. They acknowledge He is the Christ. And they deceive many. It is a sad time for the church. Packs of wolves enter pulpits across the world. Adding to this picture is 2 Timothy 3:13 where we are told: "But evil men and impostors will grow worse and worse, deceiving and being deceived." The source of these deceptions is demonic.

Now the Spirit expressly says that in latter times some will depart from the faith, giving heed to deceiving spirits and doctrines of demons, [2] speaking lies in hypocrisy, having their own conscience seared with a hot iron, [3] forbidding to marry, and commanding to abstain from foods which God created to be received with thanksgiving by those who believe and know the truth. 1 Timothy 4

"Deceiving spirits and doctrines of demons" will have their own ministry. Sewing confusion into the church. Then there are those who will merchandize their flocks. Fleecing them for all they can to build bigger homes for themselves and church buildings for their egos. The Apostle Peter spoke to that in scathing terms.

[1] But there were also false prophets among the people, even as there will be false teachers among you, who will secretly bring in destructive heresies, even denying the Lord who bought them, and bring on themselves swift destruction. [2] And many will follow their destructive ways, because of whom the way of truth will be blasphemed. [3] By covetousness they will exploit you with deceptive words; for a long time their judgment has not been idle, and their destruction does not slumber. 2 Peter 2:1-3

Jesus had a special approach to this problem as recorded in the Book of Matthew.

[12] Then Jesus went into the temple of God and drove out all those who bought and sold in the temple, and overturned the tables of the money changers and the seats of those who sold doves. [13] And He said to them, "It is written, 'My house shall be called a house of prayer,' but you have made it a 'den of thieves.' " Matthew 21:12-13

In the process of merchandizing their church, some will go as far as to claim that gifts of the Holy Spirit can be purchased. It was Peter who cleared up any questions on that topic.

> [18] And when Simon saw that through the laying on of the apostles' hands the Holy Spirit was given, he offered them money, [19] saying, "Give me this power also, that anyone on whom I lay hands may receive the Holy Spirit." [20] But Peter said to him, "Your money perish with you, because you thought that the gift of God could be purchased with money! [21] You have neither part nor portion in this matter, for your heart is not right in the sight of God. [22] Repent therefore of this your wickedness, and pray God if perhaps the thought of your heart may be forgiven you. [23] For I see that you are poisoned by bitterness and bound by iniquity." Acts 8:18-23

As the character of men descends into the abyss he is empowered by dramatic advances in technology. A bad combination. If ever there was a generation that need not be empowered by technology it is this one. As such these advances will be turned on their head. Advances that could have benefited mankind will be used to enslave him. Daniel wrote about these advances.

> "But you, Daniel, shut up the words, and seal the book until the time of the end; many shall run to and fro, and knowledge shall increase." Daniel 12:4

In Revelation 11 technology of mass media is implied by the fact that the entire world is able to see the "two witnesses" lying on a street in Jerusalem. Dead for three and a half days as the world watches.

⁹ Then those from the peoples, tribes, tongues, and nations will see their dead bodies three-and-a-half days, and not allow their dead bodies to be put into graves.

Mass media technology is necessary in order to fulfill that prophecy. And its power will rest in the worst hands possible. The godless. Major media outlets purge their ranks so only godless men remain. Because the masses must be controlled a free press cannot be allowed. With a controlled media, the dark side possesses the ability to promote not only their godless agendas but to instill twisted thinking into the minds of people creating legions of useful idiots for the Antichrist. As the time of the end approaches great power to destroy must be available. That is because Daniel tells us:

²³ "Thus he said: 'The fourth beast shall be
A fourth kingdom on earth,
Which shall be different from all other kingdoms,
And shall devour the whole earth,
Trample it and break it in pieces. Daniel 7

Conquering the world will take a new form of military power. A power so great it can bring entire nations to their knees. The splitting of the atom accomplished that task. In the language of ancient man, 2 Peter 3 describes details that can only be a nuclear detonation.

¹⁰ But the day of the Lord will come as a thief in the night, in which the heavens will pass away with a great noise, and the elements will melt with fervent heat; both the earth and the works that are in it will be burned up. ¹¹ Therefore, since all these things will be dissolved, what manner of persons ought you to be in holy conduct and godliness, ¹² looking for and hastening the coming of the day of God, because of which the heavens will be

> dissolved, being on fire, and the elements will melt with
> fervent heat? 2 Peter 3

Upon detonating there is a "great noise," in the sky the "heavens will be dissolved, being on fire, and the elements will melt with fervent heat," and near the fireball "the elements will melt with fervent heat; both the earth and the works that are in it will be burned up." But there is a problem. Since the world bristles with nuclear weapons, no nation dares strike another due to the assurance that they will equally be destroyed. This doctrine of men is called M.A.D. Mutually Assured Destruction. But the Antichrist is the master of dark sentences and deception. He has dark understanding on a level no previous leader ever had. He strikes the nations from within their own borders according to Isaiah 10. Upon such an act of war to whom do his victims strike back against? They surrender to save more cities from certain destruction in the day of great darkness. For all of this to be accomplished there must be mass uncontrolled migration into Western nations setting the stage for their own downfall.

In the second half of the seven years, when the sixth bowl judgment is poured, it dries up the river Euphrates. This is for one purpose. "So that the way of the kings from the east might be prepared." And this means that the Eastern powers have a mighty military ready to take on the Western powers for the first time in history. With the empowerment of China in recent years through free trade and technology transfers the Western powers have brought about the rise of a giant. Ready to fulfill its role in Bible prophecy.

At some point within the day of the Lord, there will be instituted a system of complete economic control. An all-encompassing system where no one will be allowed to buy or sell unless it is approved by the government of the Antichrist. Such a system will require a massive accounting ledger able to identify every person on earth. Computers.

> [16] He causes all, both small and great, rich and poor, free
> and slave, to receive a mark on their right hand or on their

foreheads, [17] and that no one may buy or sell except one who has the mark or the name of the beast, or the number of his name. [18] Here is wisdom. Let him who has understanding calculate the number of the beast, for it is the number of a man: His number is 666. Revelation 13

Not only will mankind be required to be within this economic system, but it is a system that is directly associated with the Antichrist. Everyone will be required to possess the symbol representative of the beast in order to go shopping for goods and services. It is demonic. Intimately attaching people to the devil's agent allowing end time soul harvesting to take place on a massive scale. Here are the consequences for those deceived enough to take this mark.

[9] Then a third angel followed them, saying with a loud voice, "If anyone worships the beast and his image, and receives his mark on his forehead or on his hand, [10] he himself shall also drink of the wine of the wrath of God, which is poured out full strength into the cup of His indignation. He shall be tormented with fire and brimstone in the presence of the holy angels and in the presence of the Lamb. [11] And the smoke of their torment ascends forever and ever; and they have no rest day or night, who worship the beast and his image, and whoever receives the mark of his name." Revelation 14

Exactly what this wretched mark is we can only ponder. But it very likely involves some form of technology to verify both authenticity and available funds on a mass scale. This technology is now readily available for the first time in human history.

As mankind's technology advances to the point of enabling a multitude of end time prophecy to unfold his morals and ethics have imploded alongside those advances. Although all of these prophetic developments are significant there is another one that is even more so. The state of Israel. God's prophetic time-piece. The reconstitution of that ancient nation in the year 1948 started the clock ticking. Ezekiel spoke about this in his "Valley of Dry Bones" verses. The disappearance of the Jewish nation in 70 A.D. left the Chosen People without a nation for two thousand years. Finding refuge in many different parts of the world. Experiencing terrible pogroms and persecutions just as was foretold by the prophets. Ezekiel compares the lifeless remains of Israel to "dry bones."

> ¹The hand of the LORD came upon me and brought me out in the Spirit of the LORD, and set me down in the midst of the valley; and it was full of bones. ² Then He caused me to pass by them all around, and behold, there were very many in the open valley; and indeed they were very dry. ³ And He said to me, "Son of man, can these bones live?"
>
> So I answered, "O Lord GOD, You know."
>
> ⁴ Again He said to me, "Prophesy to these bones, and say to them, 'O dry bones, hear the word of the LORD! ⁵ Thus says the Lord GOD to these bones: "Surely I will cause breath to enter into you, and you shall live. ⁶ I will put sinews on you and bring flesh upon you, cover you with skin and put breath in you; and you shall live. Then you shall know that I am the LORD." ' Ezekiel 37

The condition of Israel was nothing but dry bones. The Jewish people were scattered across the world. And their former homeland in the Middle East region, called Palestine, became occupied by polyglot nomadic tribes. Although the possibility of coming back as a nation again appeared hopeless, God had a different plan. Because to fulfill a multitude of end time prophecy scriptures they would have to exist as a nation again. Then the Lord tells Ezekiel this:

> [7] So I prophesied as I was commanded; and as I prophesied, there was a noise, and suddenly a rattling; and the bones came together, bone to bone. [8] Indeed, as I looked, the sinews and the flesh came upon them, and the skin covered them over; but there was no breath in them.

> [9] Also He said to me, "Prophesy to the breath, prophesy, son of man, and say to the breath, 'Thus says the Lord GOD: "Come from the four winds, O breath, and breathe on these slain, that they may live." ' " [10] So I prophesied as He commanded me, and breath came into them, and they lived, and stood upon their feet, an exceedingly great army. Ezekiel 37

The amazing return of the Jewish nation represents the only people group from antiquity to be so reconstitute into a nation-state again. And then other prophecies began fulfilling. As part of the Divine plan to bring back Israel, the Lord kept the land arid and unfertile. As such it was sparsely populated and not desired by any nation. The British who attained it as booty after World War One found it ungovernable and unprofitable. As such they were more than willing to divide it among the people living there according to the density of their populations. However, after the division and Israel was back in existence again another unlikely prophecy began to be fulfilled.

> [34] The desolate land shall be tilled instead of lying desolate in the sight of all who pass by. [35] So they will say, 'This land that was desolate has become like the garden of Eden; and the wasted, desolate, and ruined cities are now fortified and inhabited.' [36] Then the nations which

are left all around you shall know that I, the LORD, have
rebuilt the ruined places and planted what was desolate. I,
the LORD, have spoken it, and I will do it." Ezekiel 36

Israel became the green thumb of the Middle East. Setting an example
for the entire region. Although this is attributed to agricultural science it
was foretold by Ezekiel long ago.

And the rest is history.

A Prophetic Dream

A s the borders of the West remain wide open without regard for who is entering, the number of those coming in to do harm grows by the day. Individuals willing to fly planes into skyscrapers, or empty a magazine full of bullets into unsuspecting crowds whose only crime is not following their religion. And if those who flew the planes came in legally, how much more danger lurks from those never identified? Sent through the porous borders from enemy nations with an assigned military task. Yet, those whose hands are on the levers of power appear oblivious to the growing danger. Some even demonstrate twisted thinking. And, scariest of all, traitors in power are actual accomplices this approaching great crime.

The prophets have much to say about the days leading up to the sudden destruction that launches the day of the Lord. And none of it is good. The wealthiest nations and seemingly most secure are taken down hard. Conquered by the Antichrist going about conquering and to conquer during its birth pangs beginning. Conquered by dark sentences and crafty deceit at a level only the *beast* can muster. The prophet Isaiah tells us the fatal blow comes from such people.

They come from a far country,
From the end of heaven
The Lord and His weapons of indignation. Isaiah 13:5

Do not be thrown off by that "end of heaven" phrase. As was previously mentioned that phrase refers to events on the earth and not heaven proper. These are not angels working the wrath of the Lord. But angry men who later must "flee to [their] own land." As it happens the Lord has provided me a prophetic dream relating to this "sudden destruction" launching birth pangs. And that is the reason for this epilogue.

Please know that I understand the impact of such dreams on those being told is far less than on the one who receives them. This is understandable. It is especially true since there are so many false prophecies today from those claiming to have received dreams and visions from the Lord. We live in a time where great discernment is required. This unfortunate condition is in line with Jesus' warning at the beginning of His Olivet Discourse (MT 24:4-5). Therein He tells us the days leading up to the launch of the day of the Lord will be ones of great deceit. And who is primarily responsible for this deceit? It is those coming in His name and acknowledging He is Christ. It is from elements within the church. But in spite of all the deceit the gift of prophecy will be granted prior to the beginning of the day of the Lord. The prophet Joel says:

"And it shall come to pass afterward
That I will pour out My Spirit on all flesh;
Your sons and your daughters shall prophesy,
Your old men shall dream dreams,
Your young men shall see visions.
Joel 2:28

The gift of prophecy is given in the form of "dreams" and "visions." It is His grace and mercy as the most difficult time in human history approaches. Through the Spirit of the Lord "old men shall dream dreams."

As for young men, they too will have their part as watchmen. They "shall see visions." And as the end times draw closer with the dawn of each morning, Christians are reporting prophetic dreams and visions they believe are directly from the Lord. But discernment must be employed. Scripture cannot be added to. But details of approaching events are given through dreams and visions according to Joel.

This author is the recipient of one such dream and it directly relates to the launch of the day of the Lord. That is why I am sharing it. Since becoming a believer I have received several prophetic dreams that I know were from the Lord. Confirmation came not only in their fulfillment but the unique nature of each dream. They are remembered in detail for many years, unlike natural dreams. Here is a brief run-down of those dreams. The first came in the middle of the night on the evening I came to Christ. It drew me to Him in a very supernatural way. Although not prophetic in nature its uniqueness became seared in my memory and is only comparable to the prophetic dreams that later followed. It was different from any prior dream I had ever had. Although the first dream was used to bring me to salvation, each of the following five dreams was prophetic in nature. Of those five there are four that have come to pass. It is the fifth prophetic dream which is the subject of this epilogue and is yet to be fulfilled.

That fifth dream was extremely specific. It was not filled with hazy symbolism wherein one must guess a meaning. But spelled out with complete clarity allowing only one understanding. And that is part of its disturbing nature. But only part. The other part was the way in which the Lord answered a prayer concerning a particular detail that was not revealed in the dream. But was of the utmost importance. Here is the story.

I was clearly shown in a prophetic dream from the Lord the detonation of two nuclear weapons within the United States. I was shown the state where it will happen. I was shown the general areas within that state where each will detonate. I was even shown the order of detonations. The dream also informed me as to the method used to accomplish the attack. How were such specific details relayed? I simply watched as the dream delivered its frightening message. Having received prior prophetic dreams from the Lord, all of which came to pass, this one shook me to my core.

Every significant detail pertaining to the approaching event was given to me except for one. When it will take place? So upon that question, I began praying. For a period of about two months I prayed the same prayer each evening just before going to bed: "Lord, I pray You will tell me when this terrible day will happen." The prayer was for both curiosities as well as necessity. Not knowing the timing of this event I began thinking about what steps to take on a personal level. Should I stock up on food and other essentials? Should I begin alerting others? These were only some of the considerations that presented themselves. After praying for about 60 days a word of knowledge from the Lord came to me in the most amazing way.

Dreams from the Lord

The first dream from the Lord came in the year 1994 on the night I was saved. It was a dream of a dragon pursuing me with the intention of my destruction. After being awakened by the dream I accepted Jesus as my Savior. And the uniqueness of the dream became seared in my memory.

The next dream took place a couple of years later and was a warning of two devastating events that were heading toward me that could destroy my life. In the dream, I was shown that the Lord would block both of those events from happening. The dream possessed the same unique quality as the first one. As such I knew it was from Him. As the years passed I was able to identify those two events that fortunately did not take place.

The third dream involved a minor warning pertaining to something my youngest son Paul was involved in. At the time he was 12 years old. The results unfolded as foretold. This dream had the same unique quality as the others before it. Why something so minor was given I do not know.

The fourth dream involved another detailed warning to me personally. Like the previous dreams from the Lord, this one too possessed those same unique qualities. The specific details of the dream were fulfilled as foretold.

The fifth dream related to a unique event in business that was approaching. A literal deluge of business was indicated as approaching. Why something of this nature was given to me I do not know. But it unfolded with accuracy. This dream was actually given after the dream concerning the nuclear attack. I mention it as the fifth dream because its context relates to me on a personal level just like the other four. The dream concerning the nuclear attack stands out because it relates to an approaching major world event.

I simply relay these five dreams for no purpose other than as an accurate representation of my experience with dreams from the Lord. That is why I did not relate much detail associated with them. You can place whatever level of credibility you wish upon them. Or none at all. That is up to you. However, the dream I am about to relay impacts every person in America as well as the world. Due to my past experiences with such dreams, I believe that it will happen just as shown. I say this not only because this prophetic dream was of the same unique nature as the ones before it, but also because of the unique way in which my prayers concerning the timing of it were answered. The answering of that prayer adds another dimension of credibility to the entire affair.

Destruction on the East Coast of Florida

The dream came in the morning hours of January 23, 2009. From a bird's eye view I was allowed to see two small airplanes flying across central Florida toward its eastern coast. As I continued to watch I noticed that one of the planes veered on a southerly course along the inland coast. I was then given to see that the other plane went east toward the area of Cape Canaveral. It too stayed inland and not over the Atlantic. My attention was then directed back toward the plane that had turned south. Exactly how far south it had gone I could not see. As my gaze was fixed on it I saw the sudden detonation of a nuclear weapon. The sight of the detonation included the typical ruthless swirling waves of fire forming a massive fireball — the distinct signature of a nuclear weapon. Then my attention was immediately focused on the other plane flying toward Cape Canaveral.

I could see that the northern plane was located just south of the Cape when another nuclear detonation took place. Once again the classic fireball associated with the dreaded bomb was as vivid as the first. In line with all other dreams from the Lord, this one became etched into my memory.

Knowing the dream was from the Lord presented me with the prospect of what to do with this knowledge. As a result, I began a process of discussing it with certain friends and family members. But, understandably the impact on myself was much greater than on the ones who heard about it from me. This was especially true since I had not shared my previous dreams and their fulfillments with others. However, from the dream alone I did not know when this approaching day of infamy would take place. That answer would come through prayer and the most unusual spiritual moment of my life.

Not having any clue as to when this terrible event was to unfold was very disturbing. As a result I began pondering certain questions: Do I start preparing for the worst? How urgently do I begin informing people? As a result, of these and other questions, I began praying to the Lord for the knowledge of when it would happen. I prayed that prayer for about 60 days. And then the answer was given to me.

It was a Friday evening and as I was about to retire for the day I once again prayed the same request: "Lord, I pray you would reveal to me when this terrible day will happen." I then went to bed and slept well.

The next morning when I awoke my mind was focused on the various activities of the day. It was a Saturday morning. As I lay awake in bed considering my day something in the bedroom began to change.

I became aware of a strong spiritual presence in the room that can only be described as intense goodness. And the intensity of this goodness increased for about 30 seconds until it reached a crescendo. Then I heard the quiet still voice of the Lord speak to my heart the following words: "When they say, Peace." It was delivered with complete clarity. Thereafter, I could sense that the goodness permeating the room began to dissipate until a very short time later it was completely gone. I continued in bed for a moment pondering what had just happened.

Having never experienced anything like that I had no prior reference point to draw upon. As I lay there wondering what had just happened, I began to realize that the Lord had just answered my plea for knowledge on when the nuclear attacks against the United States would happen. It also began to dawn on me that the word of knowledge came straight from scripture.

When they say Peace

As we previously looked at in 1 Thessalonians 5:1-3 Paul informs us that the launch of the day of the Lord comes only after "they say, Peace." And this is a definitive statement of prophetic truth. He also informs us the beginning will arrive with sudden destruction. Then we looked at 2 Peter 3 wherein we are given a glimpse of this destruction. It comes not only "as a thief in the night," but will include "a great noise, and the elements shall melt with fervent heat." Once again that description.

> [10] But the day of the Lord will come as a thief in the night; in the which the heavens shall pass away with a great noise, and the elements shall melt with fervent heat, the earth also and the works that are therein shall be burned up. [11] Seeing then that all these things shall be dissolved, what manner of persons ought ye to be in all holy conversation and godliness, [12] Looking for and hasting unto the coming of the day of God, wherein the heavens being on fire shall be dissolved, and the elements shall melt with fervent heat? 2 Peter 3:10-12

The description is unmistakably that of nuclear detonations at the beginning of the day of the Lord. And who is setting off these nuclear weapons in this birth pangs beginning of the day of the Lord? As we looked at earlier according to the prophet Isaiah it is from people who represent a kind of Trojan horse within the nations that are attacked.

> 5 They come from a far country, from the end of heaven,
> even the LORD, and the weapons of his indignation, to
> destroy the whole land. Isaiah 13:5

The Antichrist attacks powerful nations from within to bring them to their knees. This is because he cannot overcome them with a direct assault. All of the attacks are directed against nations with "fenced cities, and against the high towers" — a description of the strongest military powers in the world. Here too the United States qualifies. We are also told this.

> 18 Neither their silver nor their gold shall be able to deliver
> them in the day of the LORD's wrath; but the whole land
> shall be devoured by the fire of his jealousy: for he shall
> make even a speedy riddance of all them that dwell in the
> land. Zephaniah

The nations "devoured by fire" are also very wealthy. Although they have silver and gold it is not enough to deliver them. Here too the United States qualifies. Although the United States is very powerful it has also allowed within its walls those who mean it harm. A good example of this is the September 11, 2001 hijackers. All entered the U.S. legally with the intent of doing great harm.

The revelation brought forth by the dream is a significant one. But it also led to something else. The message of the dream led this author to an understanding of end time prophecy scriptures that had previously been elusive. The road to understanding the interlocking scriptures found within these pages spans ten years. Over that time the Lord gently guided me into an understanding of how the multitude of prophecy scriptures fit together. And this was done without any regard to the customs, theories, or doctrines of men.

END TIME FLOW CHART

I. Three Major Pre-Birth Pangs Events. Birth pangs that launch the end times and not the general birth pangs so observable and growing.

The Notable War

The prophet Joel tells us there will be a notable war associated with "wonders in the heavens." This is the first sign foretelling the imminent and sudden start of birth pangs — the beginning phase of the day of the Lord. Based on a simplistic reading of scripture it is understood that the day of the Lord is the end times from start to finish. Birth pangs are simply its beginning phase coming before the seven years launch.

These "wonders" are viewed by men on earth as some kind of miracle in the heavens. This unusual sign allows that war to be identified as the one indicated by Joel. More information on this war can be found in Jesus' Olivet Discourse. Particularly in the division of verses 6-8 in Matthew 24. Therein by default, it appears that Israel is the one who is involved in those "wars and rumors of wars" found in verse 6 instead of the nations at large. And those wars and rumors of wars also occur just before the end times begin which places them in the same time frame as the notable war of Joel 2:30. This makes it likely Joel's notable war is associated with those wars and rumors of wars and involves Israel. Joel's notable war may also be the war that brings an end to the rumors and be the final war relating to Israel in the pre-birth pangs phase.

Since by default it appears the wars and rumors of wars in Matthew 24:6 must apply to Israel this brings us to the need for some speculation. Since her prophesized rebirth as a nation in the year 1948 Israel has engaged in more warfare than any other nation on earth perfectly fulfilling the wars part of the verse. But what about the rumors of wars part? That too would need to be fulfilled by the Jewish state for these verses to apply to Israel. And, indeed, Israel has been fulfilling that part as well with the help of the nation of Iran. A nation openly dedicated to the destruction of Israel. All rumors of wars between the two nations have always included the Iranian proxy allies on the Israeli northern and southern borders fulfilling the plural nature of the verse.

If this speculation is correct then it places an Israel-Iran war at center stage as a major sign of the approaching end times. Should such a war take place it would be Israel attacking the Iranian nuclear sites to disable them. And here is where another part of the prophecy appears to fit. Due to many of the Iranian nuclear facilities being built under mountains of granite, it is almost impossible to destroy them. Except for the use of one weapon. A tactical nuclear bomb. And the "pillars of smoke" indicated in Joel 2:30 appear to indicate the use of such a weapon in the notable war. This is indicated by the Greek word "timar" used to describe those pillars. "Timar" indicates a pillar of smoke with a spreading out at the top like that of a palm tree. Perfectly describing the mushroom cloud that remains in the aftermath of a nuclear detonation.

An Israeli attack on the Iranian nuclear sites using tactical nuclear weapons, associated with some kind of unusual heavenly phenomenon, would almost certainly indicate the countdown to the end times has actually begun. (Joel 2:30, Matthew 24:7-8)

The Peace Agreement

In response to such a notable war and the likely use of tactical nuclear weapons by Israel, "all nations" (The United Nations) would take action against the despised Jewish state. One response would be to initiate a "Peace" agreement removing land from them for the creation of a Palestinian state. An abomination placed in the heart of the Promised Land effectively reversing the promise of the Lord of that land to Israel. This is something the U.N. has been pressing to do for decades and will finally possess the political support to get done.

This agreement, or "covenant with many" as Daniel the prophet calls it, is the one that eventually the Antichrist "shall confirm …for one week" launching the seven years. However, his confirming will only take place after the birth pangs beginning phase of the end times is complete. Birth pangs launch from the initial agreement made by all nations — the seven-years launch from the Antichrist confirming that agreement.

Additional support that it is all nations who initiate this initial agreement comes from various prophets. Joel speaks of all nations removing land from Israel just before the end times begin without any reference to warfare as the method used to achieve it. Jeremiah 30 infers the same. Paul in 1 Thessalonians 5 specifically refers to Peace as ringing out just before the end times begin referencing the same initial agreement. He talks about those imposing it in the plural — they and them — all nations. This initial Peace agreement is the second major pre-birth pangs event indicating its launch is near. (Joel 3:1-3, 1 Thess. 5:1-3, Jeremiah 30, Daniel 9:27)

The Sun to Darkness & the Moon to Blood

"The sun shall be turned into darkness, and the moon into blood." This likely comes after the Peace agreement and appears to be the final warning that the day of the Lord is about to begin. The end times. Exactly what form this takes we do not know. But after the first two take place this one should be easily identifiable. (Joel 2:31, Acts 2:20)

II. Birth Pangs

It is clearly understood that prophetic birth pangs represent the beginning of what is popularly called the end times. There is no beginning before birth pangs. And we are told the sudden destruction beginning of the day of the Lord is birth pangs. This makes it clear that the beginning of the day of the Lord is the beginning of the end times. (1 Thessalonians 5:1-3)

The Four Horsemen of the Apocalypse

The birth pangs beginning of the end times is sudden and extraordinarily destructive including the four horsemen of the Apocalypse according to the prophet John. According to the prophet Joel, all nations are brought into the "Valley of Jehoshaphat" in judgment during birth pangs. They suffer their "full end" as described by Jeremiah and are ripe for conquering. This punishment is triggered when all nations remove the Biblical Promised Land from Israel just prior to the birth pangs beginning. Effectively attempting to reverse the promise of God to the Jews. In His Olivet Discourse Jesus identifies a great rising up of nations to warfare against each other as birth pangs launch. This great war results in great famines, pestilences and earthquakes.

Since it is referred to as birth pangs then the destructiveness of this beginning phase of the day of the Lord (the end times) likely increases in intensity as it unfolds. But its beginning is sudden. This beginning phase of the day of the Lord may last one year as it leads into the seven-years period. That seven-year time frame begins when the Antichrist confirms the initial agreement by all nations for a period of seven years. This time frame represents the seven-year tribulation. (1 Thess. 5:1-3, Matthew 24:7-8, Jeremiah 30, Revelation 6, Isaiah 34:8)

Cosmic Terror

Adding to the wars, famines, pestilences and mega earthquakes during birth pangs is a celestial terror. And it is terrifyingly visible for all to see. Exactly what form this takes requires speculation. However, based on a common-sense reading of the sixth seal it appears the most likely candidate is a massive asteroid passing very close to the Earth. This near miss brings down showers of meteors across the planet as it distorts the gravitational field of the world causing mega earthquakes and raging seas across the surface.

The Antichrist Conquers

As birth pangs unfold the Antichrist rises by "conquering and to conquer" riding the "white horse" of Revelation 6 as greater powers are brought to their knees during this time. The events of Revelation chapter 6 broadly match birth pangs. As the master of dark sentences and understandings, he takes down the most powerful nations from within using people living within the attacked nations. It is those from faraway lands who set their host nations on fire according to Isaiah. According to 2 Peter, this sudden attack likely involves the use of nuclear weapons smuggled within the Western block nations through their open borders. The prophet goes on to point out that after the attack the populations of those countries strike back against the ethnic/religious group whose members engaged in the attack. This drives them back to their faraway lands. (Revelation 6, Jeremiah 30, Joel 3, Isaiah 13)

III. The Seven Year Tribulation

After the birth pangs beginning of the day of the Lord, its next phase begins. The seventh week of Daniel is also known as the seven-year tribulation. Both birth pangs and the seven years make up the day of the Lord. The time of God's wrath. The end times.

The First Half of the Seven Years

The seven-year tribulation is the final week of years in Daniel's famous 70-weeks prophecy. (Daniel 9:20-27) It is divided into two parts. The first half encompasses the sounding of seven trumpet judgments recorded in the Book of Revelation. These judgments are severe and last until the midpoint of the seven years. As they unfold other prophetic events are taking place as well. During this time it is likely the Jewish temple is rebuilt based on a reading of Revelation 11. What we know is that it must be in place before the midpoint is reached in order for the Antichrist to defile it with his presence. And this knowledge also tells us that the Antichrist controls the City of Jerusalem at the midpoint. During this time 144,000 saved Jews are witnessing the truth of Jesus Christ to their brethren. The first stage of the salvation of Israel has begun. There are also two very unusual figures preaching in Jerusalem for the Lord at this time. They have the power to defend themselves from attack as well as afflict the earth with more plagues. When their testimony is complete the Lord allows them to be "killed." However, they rise again in three days as a supernatural rebuke to the enemies of God. (Revelation Chapters 8-11)

The Second Half of the Seven Years

The second half of the seven years unleashes the seven bowl judgments. This causes a time of destruction and death worse than any since there was a nation on the earth. It launches after the Antichrist defiles the rebuilt

Jewish temple by sitting in it and pretending to be a god. Thereafter, he requires every man, woman and child on the earth to worship him as such. Those who refuse are killed usually by beheading. It is during this time that mystery Babylon rages in her corrupt fullness. Exactly what city represents this whore is debated. However, her seamy hands drip with the blood of the martyrs. Sometime during this second half, the 144,000 Jews who have been witnessing to their fellow Jews are gone from the earth. They are found in heaven singing to the Lord. Exactly how they get there is an open question. They are described as first fruits of a coming harvest. And that harvest appears several verses later wherein Jesus appears on a cloud to take it. Revelation 14 is a simplistic chapter presenting six notable second half events each kept separate by announcing angels. Sometime during the second half the Jews retake the City of Jerusalem from the Antichrist. We know this by the fact that Antichrist must gather a great army to re-take Judah and Jerusalem from the Jews. The loss of Jerusalem is the lure that brings the Antichrist and his armies to the Battles of Armageddon, Judah and Jerusalem. These great battles take place at the end of the seven years. During these battles, God supernaturally empowers the Jews to overcome tremendous odds. He also makes His glorious appearance causing the Chosen People to realize that they killed their messiah years earlier. This realization comes after years of preaching to Israel from the 144,000 that Jesus is the Christ and their Savior. After these battles, the end times are over. Then starts the thousand-year reign of Christ on the earth. Thereafter, the guilty are judged for their sins.

ADDENDUMS

Addendum 1: Why the Assyrian must be the Antichrist

Isaiah 31: God Will Deliver Jerusalem

[4] For thus hath the LORD spoken unto me, Like as the lion and the young lion roaring on his prey, when a multitude of shepherds is called forth against him, he will not be afraid of their voice, nor abase himself for the noise of them: so shall the LORD of hosts come down to fight for mount Zion, and for the hill thereof. — Second Coming

[5] As birds flying, so will the LORD of hosts defend Jerusalem; defending also he will deliver it; and passing over he will preserve it.

[6] Turn ye unto him from whom the children of Israel have deeply revolted.

[7] For in that day every man shall cast away his idols of silver, and his idols of gold, which your own hands have made unto you for a sin.

[8] Then shall <u>the Assyrian</u> fall with the sword, not of a mighty man; and the sword, not of a mean man, shall devour him: but he shall flee from the sword, and his young men shall be discomfited.

[9] And he shall pass over to his strong hold for fear, and <u>his princes</u> shall be afraid of the ensign, (BANNER) saith the LORD, whose fire is in Zion, and his furnace in Jerusalem.

Addendum 2: Why the correct reading of 2 Thessalonians 2:2 must be "the day of Christ" and not "the day of the Lord."

The difference in readings is based on old manuscripts in which some read "the day of Christ" and others "the day of the Lord." And in the case that it reads "the day of the Lord" then Paul's words are not useful as a prophetic perspective on the resurrection & rapture. Several good Bible versions such as the American Standard Bible, the International Standard Version, the New American Standard Bible and others read "the day of the Lord" instead of "the day of Christ." However, King James, New King James and others read "the day of Christ."

But there is a way to know which old manuscript relays it correctly. That is because if it reads "the day of the Lord," instead of "the day of Christ," then two irreconcilable scriptural conflicts arise with Paul's previous words. Here is how.

By reading the passage as "the day of the Lord," then the verses in question have Paul correcting the Thessalonians for thinking that "the day of the Lord" has already come. This places the Thessalonian church with the dubious distinction of being in error concerning the start of "the day of the Lord." And it shows them lacking in a basic understanding of the start of "the day of the Lord." Now here is the conflict. Two chapters earlier Paul is congratulating the Thessalonians on their knowledge of the start of "the day of the Lord." Consider the verses in question:

> But concerning the times and the seasons, brethren, you
> have no need that I should write to you. ² For you your-
> selves know perfectly that the day of the Lord so comes
> as a thief in the night. ³ For when they say, "Peace and
> safety!" then sudden destruction comes upon them, as
> labor pains upon a pregnant woman. And they shall not
> escape. ⁴ But you, brethren, are not in darkness, so that
> this Day should overtake you as a thief. ⁵ You are all sons

of light and sons of the day. We are not of the night nor of darkness. ⁶Therefore let us not sleep, as others do, but let us watch and be sober. 1 Thessalonians 5:1-6

Paul starts by acknowledging the Thessalonians "perfectly know" about the start of "the day of the Lord." And he says their knowledge is so good that he has "no need that I should write to you" about it because they already understand. And, therefore, it will not "overtake" them since they are aware and not in "darkness." This is a strikingly different assessment of their understanding concerning the start of "the day of the Lord" than indicated two chapters later if "the day of the Lord" manuscript is used. But there is a second conflict as well.

Reading the passages in question as "the day of the Lord" has Paul pointing out that the Antichrist must first sit in the temple before "the day of the Lord" starts. That places "the day of the Lord" as beginning in the second half of the seven years. But the passages in 1 Thessalonians 5 address that as well.

In 1 Thessalonians 5:1-3 Paul tells the Thessalonians that the "sudden destruction" launching "the day of the Lord" represents birth pangs — the "beginning" of the end times and not the mid-point. And we know prophetic birth pangs launch the end times and do not take place after the midpoint. Since there is no debate relating to the use of the phrase "the day of the Lord" in 1 Thessalonians 5:1-3, then this is another strike against the manuscripts indicating that 2 Thessalonians 2:2 reads "the day of the Lord" instead of "the day of Christ." Now here is strike three.

2 Thessalonians 2:2 starts by telling us: "Now, brethren, concerning the coming of our Lord Jesus Christ and our gathering together to Him, we ask you..." And this is clearly a description of the resurrection & rapture and not "the day of the Lord." So for these reasons, the manuscript reading "the day of Christ" makes more sense and supports that the resurrection & rapture do not take place until sometime within the second half of the seven years. And this is in agreement with the other prophets.

Addendum 3: Pre-Tribulation Rapture Points & Counter Points

Because of the sensitive nature of this topic, it is necessary to address points made by those claiming the resurrection & rapture take place much earlier than indicated by the prophets. Point by point here are some of their claims.

Point 1: We must be raptured before God's wrath begins.

There are those who say, that since the saved are not subject to the wrath of God, therefore, they must be raptured before His wrath begins. And at first glance, this seems to have merit. But they take an absolute Biblical truth, "the saved are not subject to the wrath of God," and draw a wrong conclusion. Because it ignores the fact that the Lord can protect His children as His wrath rains down around them. There are several Biblical examples of the Lord simply protecting His children as His wrath unfolds around them.

The Israelites in ancient Egypt are a prime example. As His wrath fell across the land in one plague after another not a single Jew was harmed. There is also the example of Lot and his family. They were protected from the Lord's wrath as Sodom and Gomorrah were destroyed with fire and brimstone. And there is Noah and his family. They were saved from the Lord's wrath in the form of the great flood. The Lord's protection was secure as His wrath unfolded without having to use a rapture.

In the Book of Revelation as His wrath is coming down we are told of His protection around those who are His. This is done by placing a seal on them. This is the same seal mentioned in 2 Corinthians 1 where we are told: "21 Now He who establishes us with you in Christ and has anointed us is God, 22 who also has sealed us and given us the Spirit in our hearts as a guarantee." The protective power of that seal is greater than the horrors of Revelation.

Then I saw another angel ascending from the east, having the seal of the living God. And he cried with a loud voice to the four angels to whom it was granted to harm the earth and the sea, saying, "Do not harm the earth, the sea, or the trees till we have <u>sealed</u> the servants of our God on their foreheads." Revelation 7:2-3

And...

³ Then out of the smoke locusts came upon the earth. And to them was given power, as the scorpions of the earth have power. ⁴ They were commanded not to harm the grass of the earth, or any green thing, or any tree, but only those men who do not have the <u>seal</u> of God on their foreheads. Revelation 9:3-4

The Lord's ability to protect His children is perfect amid His wrath raining down around them. He has no need to rapture those who are sealed in order to protect them. Some people then make the case that even though the Lord has the absolute power to protect His own as His wrath comes, He would never allow His children to go through such a terrible time. However, that is the flesh of man speaking and not the Spirit.

The Lord created the universe and man for one purpose. His glory. And He is best glorified when His children stand firm for Him is the face of terror. Accordingly, the end times present the season of the greatest opportunity to glorify His name across the earth. And to witness. This truth runs hard against the flesh and is difficult for some to accept. But the Bible is filled with stories of the Lord's children refusing the easy way out to His glory. In Revelation 12:11 we are told: "And they overcame him by the blood of the Lamb, and by the word of their testimony; and they loved not their lives unto the death."

These words are given as a model for believers going through the end times. They reflect a willingness on the part of His children to stand up for

Him even to the point of martyrdom. And there is no greater way for Him to be glorified by His children than this one action. In turn, His children receive benefits and are eternally grateful He allowed the opportunity to glorify Him while on Earth.

Point 2. Supporters of an early resurrection & rapture view Revelation 3:10 as indicating the removal of the church before the end times begin.

As Jesus is speaking to the church in Philadelphia He says:

> ¹⁰ Because you have kept My command to persevere, I also will keep you from the hour of trial which shall come upon the whole world, to test those who dwell on the earth. Revelation 3:10

Based on the wording in this verse some say that Jesus is telling His church that before the end times begin they will be removed (raptured). Well… not quite. The key in the verse is what is meant by "keep you from." Does it mean rapture out of or simply to protect "from the hour of trial which shall come upon the whole world." The Greek verb "tereo" is used there meaning "to attend to carefully, take care of and to guard" but not remove. Now applying the principle of using scripture to interpret itself we find a previous passage in which Jesus uses this same term, keep from ("tereo"), in excellent context with its usage in Revelation 3:11.

> ¹⁵ I do not pray that You should take them out of the world, but that You should <u>keep them from</u> the evil one. John 17:15

As can be seen Jesus is telling His disciples that instead of taking them out of the world, as in rapture, He will "tereo," attend to carefully, take care of and guard them. Since the Spirit is consistent then when reading Revelation 3:10 we see that "keep you from the hour of trial" means to protect from and not remove from the earth. The Lord will simply attend to them carefully, take care of them and guard them, just as He did for the Israelites in ancient Egypt.

Point 3. No man knows "the day or the hour" so the rapture can happen at any time.

Scripture is very clear that no man knows "the day or the hour" of the resurrection & rapture. But scripture actually means what it says. It is "the day and hour" we cannot know and not the season. In fact, as we have seen multiple prophets provide the season.

> But of the times and the seasons, brethren, ye have no need that I write unto you. ² For yourselves know perfectly that the day of the Lord so cometh as a thief in the night.³ For when they shall say, Peace and safety; then sudden destruction cometh upon them, as travail upon a woman with child; and they shall not escape.

After congratulating the Thessalonians on their awareness of the times and seasons, even saying they know the season of "the day of the Lord" perfectly, Paul goes on to stress the importance of this understanding.

> ⁴ But ye, brethren, are not in darkness, that that day should overtake you as a thief.⁵ Ye are all the children of light, and the children of the day: we are not of the night, nor of darkness.⁶ Therefore let us not sleep, as do others; but let us watch and be sober.⁷ For they that sleep sleep in the night; and they that be drunken are drunken in the night.

Paul compares those who do not know the season of "the day of the Lord" to those who are "drunken in the night." They are in "darkness" and, as a result, will be overtaken "as a thief." But since the Thessalonians are "children of light," understanding perfectly the signs coming before "the day of the Lord" begins, then they are to "watch and be sober." Interestingly, since he is telling them to "watch" for the "beginning of the day of the Lord," then for the church to see it they will have to be present when it begins. And that too is in line with the multitude of prophets who say the same.

www.ingramcontent.com/pod-product-compliance
Lightning Source LLC
Chambersburg PA
CBHW012012290326
41934CB00016BA/3451